fast
food

fast
food

MURDOCH BOOKS

Contents

Pot

Beef and chilli bean soup

1 tablespoon oil
1 red onion, finely chopped
2 cloves garlic, crushed
2½ teaspoons chilli flakes
2½ teaspoons ground cumin
2½ tablespoons finely chopped fresh
  coriander root and stem
1½ teaspoons ground coriander
500 g lean beef mince
1 tablespoon tomato paste
  (tomato purée)
4 tomatoes, peeled, seeded
  and diced
420 g can red kidney beans, drained
  and rinsed
2 litres beef stock
3 tablespoons chopped fresh
  coriander leaves
⅓ cup (80 g) sour cream

Heat the oil in a large saucepan over medium heat. Cook the onion for 2–3 minutes, or until softened. Add the garlic, chilli flakes, cumin, fresh and ground coriander, and cook for 1 minute. Add the mince and cook for 3–4 minutes, or until cooked through—break up any lumps with a spoon.

Add the tomato paste, tomato, beans and stock and bring to the boil. Reduce the heat, simmer for 15–20 minutes, or until rich and reduced slightly. Remove any scum on the surface. Stir in the chopped coriander. Serve with sour cream.

Serves 4

Scallops with soba noodles and dashi broth

250 g soba noodles
3 tablespoons mirin
¼ cup (60 ml) soy sauce
2 teaspoons rice wine vinegar
1 teaspoon dashi granules
2 spring onions, sliced on
  the diagonal
1 teaspoon finely chopped
  fresh ginger
24 large scallops (without roe)
5 fresh black fungus, chopped
1 sheet nori, shredded, to garnish

Cook the soba noodles in a large saucepan of rapidly boiling water for 5 minutes, or until tender. Drain and rinse under cold water.

Place the mirin, soy sauce, rice wine vinegar, dashi granules and 3 cups (750 ml) water in a saucepan. Bring to the boil, then reduce the heat and simmer for 3–4 minutes. Add the spring onion and ginger and keep at a gentle simmer until needed.

Heat a chargrill or hotplate until very hot and sear the scallops on both sides, in batches, for 1 minute.

Divide the noodles and black fungus among four deep serving bowls. Pour ¾ cup (185 ml) broth into each bowl and top with 6 scallops each. Garnish with the nori and serve immediately.

Serves 4

Note: If you can't buy fresh black fungus, use dried instead but soak it in warm water for 15–20 minutes before use.

Spaghettini with asparagus and rocket

100 ml extra virgin olive oil
16 thin asparagus spears, cut
  into 5 cm lengths
375 g spaghettini
120 g rocket, shredded
2 small fresh red chillies,
  finely chopped
2 teaspoons finely grated lemon rind
1 clove garlic, finely chopped
1 cup (100 g) grated Parmesan
2 tablespoons lemon juice

Bring a large saucepan of water to the boil over medium heat. Add 1 tablespoon of the oil and a pinch of salt to the water and blanch the asparagus for 3–4 minutes. Remove the asparagus with a slotted spoon, refresh under cold water, drain and place in a bowl. Return the water to a rapid boil and add the spaghettini. Cook the pasta until *al dente*. Drain and return to the pan.

Meanwhile, add the rocket, chilli, lemon rind, garlic and $2/3$ cup (65 g) of the Parmesan to the asparagus and mix well. Add to the pasta, pour on the lemon juice and remaining olive oil and season with salt and freshly ground black pepper. Stir well to evenly coat the pasta with the mixture. Divide among four pasta bowls, top with the remaining Parmesan and serve.

Serves 4

Note: You can use other types of pasta such as tagliatelle, macaroni or spiral-shaped pasta.

Orecchiette with mushrooms, pancetta and smoked mozzarella

400 g orecchiette
2 tablespoons olive oil
150 g sliced pancetta, cut into
   short thin strips
200 g button mushrooms,
   sliced
2 leeks, sliced
1 cup (250 ml) cream
200 g smoked mozzarella
   (mozzarella affumicata),
   cut into 1 cm cubes
8 fresh basil leaves, roughly torn

Cook the orecchiette in a large saucepan of rapidly boiling salted water until *al dente*.

Meanwhile, heat the oil in a large frying pan and sauté the pancetta, mushrooms and leek over medium–high heat for 5 minutes. Stir in the cream and season with pepper—the pancetta should provide enough salty flavour. Simmer over low heat for 5 minutes, or until the pasta is ready. Drain the pasta and stir into the frying pan. Add the mozzarella and basil and toss lightly.

Serves 4

Note: If you are watching your weight, you can use half chicken stock and half cream instead of all cream. Smoked provolone can be used instead of the mozzarella, if preferred.

Beef and red wine stew

1 kg diced beef
1/4 cup (30 g) seasoned plain flour
1 tablespoon oil
150 g bacon, diced
8 bulb spring onions, greens
   trimmed to 2 cm
200 g button mushrooms
2 cups (500 ml) red wine
2 tablespoons tomato paste
   (tomato purée)
2 cups (500 ml) beef stock
1 bouquet garni

Toss the beef in the seasoned flour until evenly coated, shaking off any excess. Heat the oil in a large saucepan over high heat. Cook the beef in three batches for about 3 minutes, or until well browned all over, adding a little extra oil as needed. Remove from the pan.

Add the bacon to the pan and cook for 2 minutes, or until browned. Remove with a slotted spoon and add to the beef. Add the spring onions and mushrooms and cook for 5 minutes, or until the onions are browned. Remove.

Slowly pour the red wine into the pan, scraping up any sediment from the bottom with a wooden spoon. Stir in the tomato paste and stock. Add the bouquet garni and return the beef, bacon and any juices to the pan. Bring to the boil, then reduce the heat and simmer for 45 minutes, then return the spring onions and mushrooms to the pan. Cook for 1 hour, or until the meat is very tender and the sauce is glossy. Serve with steamed new potatoes or mash.

Serves 4

Note: Although this stew takes a long time to cook, it is very quick to prepare and the result is delicious.

Pea, lettuce and bacon soup

2 tablespoons vegetable oil
2 onions, finely chopped
200 g bacon rashers, chopped
1 kg frozen baby peas, defrosted
1.5 litres chicken stock
1.2 kg iceburg lettuce,
   finely shredded
watercress sprigs, to garnish

Heat the oil in large saucepan over medium heat. Add the onion and bacon and cook for 2–3 minutes, or until soft, but not browned. Add the peas, stock and half the lettuce to the pan, then simmer for 5 minutes, or until the peas are tender. Season.

Allow the soup to cool slightly, then blend in batches until smooth. Return to the pan with the remaining lettuce and stir over medium–low heat until warmed through. Serve, garnished with the watercress.

Serves 4

Lemon thyme tuna with tagliatelle

375 g tagliatelle
140 ml extra virgin olive oil
1 small fresh red chilli, seeded
and finely chopped
1/4 cup (50 g) drained capers
1 1/2 tablespoons fresh lemon thyme
leaf tips
500 g tuna steaks, trimmed and
cut into 3 cm cubes
1/4 cup (60 ml) lemon juice
1 tablespoon grated lemon zest
1/2 cup (30 g) chopped fresh
flat-leaf parsley

Cook the tagliatelle in a large saucepan of rapidly boiling salted water until *al dente*. Drain, then return to the pan.

Meanwhile, heat 1 tablespoon of the oil in a large frying pan. Add the chilli and capers and cook, stirring, for 1 minute, or until the capers are crisp. Add the thyme and cook for another minute. Transfer to a bowl.

Heat another tablespoon of oil in the pan. Add the tuna cubes and toss for 2–3 minutes, or until evenly browned on the outside but still pink in the centre—check with the point of a sharp knife. Remove from the heat.

Add the tuna to the caper mixture along with the lemon juice, lemon rind, parsley and the remaining oil, stirring gently until combined. Toss through the pasta, season with freshly ground black pepper and serve immediately.

Serves 4

Creamy garlic prawn fettuccine

400 g fresh fettuccine
1 tablespoon olive oil
1 onion, finely chopped
3 cloves garlic, crushed
400 g tomatoes, seeded and
  chopped
¼ cup (60 ml) white wine
300 ml cream
1 kg raw medium prawns, peeled,
  deveined and tails intact
½ cup (15 g) loosely packed
  roughly chopped fresh basil

Cook the fettuccine in a large saucepan of rapidly boiling salted water until *al dente*. Drain, then return to the pan.

Heat the oil in a large frying pan over medium–high heat and cook the onion and garlic, stirring, for 4–5 minutes, or until the onion is soft. Add the tomato and wine and cook for 3 minutes before adding the cream. Bring to the boil, then reduce the heat to medium–low and simmer for 5 minutes, or until it slightly thickens. Stir in the prawns, then simmer for 3–4 minutes, or until the prawns turn pink and are curled and cooked through. Toss with the pasta, gently stir in the basil, season and serve immediately.

Serves 4

Beef masala with coconut rice

1 tablespoon oil
1 kg chuck steak, trimmed and cut
  into 2 cm cubes
1 large onion, thinly sliced
3 cloves garlic, chopped
⅓ cup (80 g) tikka masala curry paste
2 teaspoons tamarind concentrate
2 x 400 ml cans coconut milk
4 fresh curry leaves
1½ cups (300 g) jasmine rice

Heat the oil in a large saucepan over high heat. Add the meat and cook in three batches for 4 minutes per batch, or until evenly browned.

Reduce the heat to medium, add the onion to the pan, cook for 5 minutes, then add the garlic and cook for 1 minute. Stir in the curry paste and tamarind for 30–60 seconds, until fragrant. Return the beef to the pan, add 550 ml coconut milk and the curry leaves and bring to the boil. Reduce the heat and simmer gently for 1½ hours, or until the meat is tender and the sauce has reduced. Add some water if the sauce starts to stick to the base of the pan.

Meanwhile, to make the coconut rice, wash and thoroughly drain the rice. Put the rice, the remaining coconut milk and 1 cup (250 ml) water in a saucepan and bring slowly to the boil, stirring constantly. Boil for 1 minute, then reduce the heat to low and cook, covered tightly, for 20 minutes. Remove from the heat and leave, covered, for 10 minutes. Fluff the rice with a fork before serving. To serve, season to taste and remove the curry leaves if you wish. Serve with the rice.

Serves 4

Note: Beef masala takes a while to cook but the preparation time is short.

Spaghetti marinara

2 tablespoons olive oil
1 onion, finely chopped
2 cloves garlic, crushed
2 x 400 g cans diced tomatoes
¼ cup (60 g) tomato paste
  (tomato purée)
500 g spaghetti
500 g good-quality marinara mix
  (see Note)
8 black mussels, beards removed,
  scrubbed
2 tablespoons shredded fresh basil

Heat the oil in a saucepan over medium heat, add the onion and cook for 5 minutes, or until soft and golden. Add the garlic and stir for 1 minute, or until aromatic. Add the tomato and tomato paste and bring to the boil, then reduce the heat and simmer for 20–25 minutes, or until the sauce becomes rich and pulpy. Stir the sauce occasionally during cooking. Season with salt and cracked black pepper. Meanwhile, cook the spaghetti in a large saucepan of rapidly boiling water until *al dente*. Drain well, return to the saucepan and keep warm.

Add the marinara mix and the mussels to the tomato sauce and cook for about 2–3 minutes, or until the seafood is cooked and the mussels are open. Discard any mussels that don't open. Stir in the basil. Toss the sauce through the warm pasta and serve.

Serves 4–6

Note: Marinara mix is available from seafood specialists. Choose a good-quality mix to avoid chewy seafood. Alternatively, make your own by buying different types of seafood, such as octopus, fish fillets and calamari and chopping into bite-size pieces.

Buckwheat noodles with sweet and sour capsicum

3 capsicums (peppers), preferably
  red, green and yellow
2 tablespoons vegetable oil
5 teaspoons sesame oil
2 star anise
1/4 cup (60 ml) red wine vinegar
1 tablespoon fish sauce
1/2 cup (125 g) sugar
300 g buckwheat noodles
1/2 tablespoon balsamic vinegar
1/2 teaspoon sugar, extra
2 spring onions, finely sliced
2 tablespoons sesame seeds,
  lightly toasted

Thinly slice the capsicums. Heat the oil and 1 teaspoon sesame oil in a saucepan over medium heat. Cook the star anise for 1 minute, or until the oil begins to smoke. Add the capsicum and stir for 2 minutes. Reduce the heat to low and cook, covered, for 5 minutes, stirring occasionally. Increase to medium heat and add the vinegar, fish sauce and sugar, stirring until dissolved. Boil for 2 minutes, then remove from the heat and cool. Remove the star anise. Drain and place the capsicum in a bowl.

Cook the noodles in a large saucepan of rapidly boiling water for 5 minutes. Drain and rinse.

Combine the balsamic vinegar, remaining sesame oil, extra sugar and 1/2 teaspoon salt, stirring until the sugar dissolves. Add the noodles and toss to coat, then combine with the capsicum and spring onion. Sprinkle with the sesame seeds and serve.

Serves 4

Sichuan chicken

¼ teaspoon five-spice powder
750 g chicken thigh fillets, halved
2 tablespoons peanut oil
1 tablespoon julienned fresh ginger
1 teaspoon Sichuan peppercorns,
    crushed
1 teaspoon chilli bean paste
    (toban jian)
2 tablespoons light soy sauce
1 tablespoon Chinese rice wine
1¼ cups (250 g) jasmine rice
600 g baby bok choy,
    leaves separated

Sprinkle the five-spice powder over
the chicken. Heat a saucepan or wok
until very hot, add half the oil and swirl
to coat. Add the chicken and cook for
2 minutes each side, or until browned.
Remove from the pan or wok.

Reduce the heat to medium and cook
the ginger for 30 seconds. Add the
peppercorns and chilli bean paste.
Return the chicken to the pan or wok,
add the soy sauce, wine and ½ cup
(125 ml) water, then simmer for
15–20 minutes, or until cooked.

Meanwhile, add the rice to a large
saucepan of rapidly boiling water and
cook for 12 minutes, stirring
occasionally. Drain well.

Heat the remaining oil in a saucepan.
Add the bok choy and toss for
1 minute, or until the leaves wilt
and the stems are tender. Serve
with the chicken and rice.

Serves 4

Ziti carbonara

500 g ziti
1 tablespoon olive oil
200 g piece pancetta, cut into
    long thin strips
4 egg yolks
300 ml cream
½ cup (50 g) grated Parmesan
2 tablespoons finely chopped
    fresh flat-leaf parsley

Cook the pasta in a large saucepan of rapidly boiling salted water until *al dente*. Drain well and return to the pan. Meanwhile, heat the olive oil in a non-stick frying pan and cook the pancetta over high heat for 6 minutes, or until crisp and golden.

Beat the egg yolks, cream and Parmesan together in a bowl and season generously. Pour over the hot pasta in the saucepan and toss gently. Add the pancetta and parsley. Return the pan to very low heat and cook for 30–60 seconds, or until the sauce has thickened and coats the pasta. Don't cook over high heat or the eggs will scramble. Season with salt and freshly ground black pepper and serve immediately with extra Parmesan, if desired.

Serves 4–6

Pasta with pork and fennel sausages

6 Italian pork and fennel sausages
(about 550 g)
1 tablespoon olive oil
1 small red onion, finely chopped
2–3 cloves garlic, crushed
½ teaspoon chilli flakes
300 g field or button mushrooms,
thinly sliced
2 x 400 g cans diced tomatoes
1 tablespoon finely chopped
fresh thyme
500 g penne rigate
grated Parmesan, to serve

Split the sausages open, remove and crumble the filling and discard the skins.

Heat the oil in a large saucepan over medium–high heat and cook the onion for 3–4 minutes, or until fragrant and transparent. Add the garlic, chilli flakes, mushrooms and crumbled sausage meat. Cook over high heat, stirring gently to mash the sausage meat, for 4–5 minutes, or until the meat is evenly browned. If necessary, use a tablespoon to remove any excess fat from the pan, leaving about a tablespoon of oil. Continue to cook, stirring once or twice, for 10 minutes.

Stir in the tomato and thyme, then bring the sauce to the boil. Cover and cook over medium–low heat for 20 minutes, stirring occasionally to make sure the sauce doesn't stick to the bottom of the pan.

Meanwhile, cook the penne rigate in a large saucepan of rapidly boiling salted water until *al dente*. Drain well, then add to the sauce, stirring to combine. Garnish with Parmesan, then serve immediately with a green salad.

Serves 4

Note: This dish takes a while to cook but the ingredients won't take you long to prepare.

Cotelli with spring vegetables

500 g cotelli
2 cups (310 g) frozen peas
2 cups (310 g) frozen broad beans,
    blanched and peeled
⅓ cup (80 ml) olive oil
6 spring onions, cut into
    3 cm pieces
2 cloves garlic, finely chopped
1 cup (250 ml) chicken stock
12 thin fresh asparagus spears,
    cut into 5 cm lengths
1 lemon

Cook the cotelli in a large saucepan of rapidly boiling salted water until *al dente*. Drain and return to the pan. Meanwhile, cook the peas in a saucepan of boiling water for 1–2 minutes, until tender. Remove with a slotted spoon and plunge into cold water. Add the broad beans to the saucepan, cook for 1–2 minutes, then drain and plunge into cold water. Remove and slip the skins off.

Heat 2 tablespoons of the oil in a frying pan. Add the spring onion and garlic and cook over medium heat for 2 minutes, or until softened. Pour in the stock and cook for 5 minutes, or until slightly reduced. Add the asparagus and cook for 3–4 minutes, until bright green and just tender. Stir in the peas and broad beans and cook for 2–3 minutes, or until heated through.

Toss the remaining oil through the pasta, then add the vegetable mixture, ½ teaspoon finely grated lemon rind and ¼ cup (60 ml) lemon juice. Season to taste with salt and cracked black pepper and toss together well. Divide among four bowls and top with shaved Parmesan, if desired.

Serves 4

Paprika veal with caraway noodles

3 tablespoons oil
1 kg diced veal shoulder
1 large onion, thinly sliced
3 cloves garlic, finely chopped
¼ cup (60 g) Hungarian paprika
½ teaspoon caraway seeds
2 x 400 g cans chopped tomatoes,
  one drained
350 g fresh fettuccine
40 g butter, softened

Heat half the oil in a large saucepan over medium–high heat, then brown the veal in batches for 3 minutes per batch. Remove the veal from the pan and set aside with any pan juices.

Add the remaining oil to the pan and sauté the onion and garlic over medium heat for 5 minutes, or until softened. Add the paprika and ¼ teaspoon of the caraway seeds and stir for 30 seconds.

Add the chopped tomatoes and their liquid plus ½ cup (125 ml) water. Return the veal to the pan with any juices, increase the heat to high and bring to the boil. Reduce the heat to low, then cover and simmer for 1 hour 15 minutes, or until the meat is tender and the sauce has thickened.

About 15 minutes before the veal is ready, cook the pasta in a large saucepan of rapidly boiling salted water until *al dente*. Drain, then return to the pan. Stir in the butter and the remaining caraway seeds. Serve immediately with the veal.

Serves 4

Note: Although this recipe has a long cooking time, it is quick to prepare.

Tomato ditalini soup

2 tablespoons olive oil
1 large onion, finely chopped
2 celery sticks, finely chopped
3 vine-ripened tomatoes
1.5 litres chicken or vegetable stock
½ cup (90 g) ditalini
2 tablespoons chopped fresh
  flat-leaf parsley

Heat the oil in a large saucepan over medium heat. Add the onion and celery and cook for 5 minutes, or until they have softened.

Score a cross in the base of each tomato, then place them in a bowl of boiling water for 1 minute. Plunge into cold water and peel the skin away from the cross. Halve the tomatoes and scoop out the seeds. Roughly chop the flesh. Add the stock and tomato to the onion mixture and bring to the boil. Add the ditalini and cook for 10 minutes, or until *al dente*. Season and sprinkle with parsley. Serve with crusty bread.

Serves 4

Cheese tortellini with capsicum and almond sauce

1 red capsicum (pepper)
1 yellow capsicum (pepper)
2/3 cup (60 g) flaked almonds
8 spring onions
2 cloves garlic, crushed
500 g cheese tortellini
2/3 cup (170 ml) olive oil
1/3 cup (30 g) finely grated
   pecorino cheese

Cut the capsicums into large pieces, removing the seeds and membrane. Place, skin-side-up, under a hot grill until the skin blackens and blisters. Cool in a plastic bag, then peel away the skin. Spread the almonds on a grill tray and grill for 1–2 minutes, or until lightly toasted.

Roughly chop the white part of the spring onions and slice the green tops, reserving for garnish. Put the capsicum, almonds, garlic and white part of the spring onion in a food processor and pulse until chopped.

Cook the pasta in a large saucepan of boiling water until *al dente*. Drain and return to the pan. Toss the capsicum mixture through the pasta, then add the oil and cheese. Season to taste. Serve garnished with the reserved green spring onion.

Serves 4

Fresh tomato and basil sauce with pasta

400 g spaghetti
5 tablespoons extra virgin olive oil
5 cloves garlic, thinly sliced
6 vine-ripened tomatoes, seeded and chopped
3/4 cup (25 g) torn fresh basil leaves

Bring a large saucepan of water to the boil, add a pinch of salt, then add the pasta and cook according to the packet instructions, until *al dente*. Drain the pasta. If the pasta will be sitting around for a little while before being added to the sauce, return it to the pan and toss through a little olive oil to prevent it from sticking together.

While the pasta is cooking, heat 4 tablespoons of the oil in a frying pan and cook the garlic over low heat for 1 minute. As soon as the garlic begins to change colour, remove the pan from the heat and add the remaining oil.

Add the cooked pasta to the pan with the tomato and basil. Season generously with salt and ground black pepper. Toss well and serve drizzled a little extra virgin olive oil.

Serves 4

Veal agnolotti with alfredo sauce

625 g veal agnolotti
90 g butter
1½ cups (150 g) grated Parmesan
300 ml cream
2 tablespoons chopped
   fresh marjoram

Cook the veal agnolotti in a large saucepan of rapidly boiling salted water until *al dente*. Drain and return to the pan.

Just before the pasta is cooked, melt the butter in a saucepan over low heat. Add the Parmesan and cream and bring to the boil. Reduce the heat and simmer, stirring constantly, for 2 minutes, or until the sauce has thickened slightly. Stir in the marjoram and season with salt and cracked black pepper. Toss the sauce through the pasta. Serve immediately.

Serves 4–6

Note: Any fresh herb such as parsley, thyme, chervil or dill can be used instead of marjoram.

Thai green chicken curry with coriander rice

1¼ cups (250 g) jasmine rice
1 tablespoon vegetable oil
1–2 tablespoons Thai green curry paste
4 fresh kaffir lime leaves *hardly any of this!*
1 tablespoon fish sauce
2 teaspoons palm sugar
400 ml can coconut cream
750 g skinless chicken breast fillets, cut into strips (2 cm x 6 cm)
4 tablespoons roughly chopped fresh coriander leaves
2 tablespoons whole fresh coriander leaves

Bring a large saucepan of water to the boil. Add the rice and cook for 12 minutes, stirring occasionally. Drain well.

Meanwhile, heat the oil over high heat in a saucepan or wok, then add the curry paste and lime leaves and fry over medium–high heat for 1–2 minutes, or until fragrant. Add the fish sauce and palm sugar and mix well. Pour in the coconut cream, bring to the boil, then add the chicken strips. Reduce the heat to medium and simmer for 12–15 minutes, or until the sauce is reduced and the chicken is tender and cooked.

Just before serving, stir the chopped coriander through the rice. Serve the curry over the coriander rice, garnished with coriander leaves.

Serves 4

Chicken and spinach risoni soup

1 tablespoon olive oil
1 leek, quartered lengthways and
  thinly sliced
2 cloves garlic, crushed
1 teaspoon ground cumin
1.5 litres chicken stock
2 chicken breast fillets (about 500 g)
1 cup (205 g) risoni
150 g baby English spinach leaves,
  roughly chopped
1 tablespoon chopped fresh dill
2 teaspoons lemon juice

Heat the oil in a large saucepan over low heat. Add the leek and cook for 8–10 minutes, or until soft. Add the garlic and cumin and cook for 1 minute. Pour the stock into the pan, increase the heat to high and bring to the boil. Reduce the heat to low, add the chicken fillets and simmer, covered, for 8 minutes. Remove the chicken from the broth, allow to cool slightly, then shred.

Stir the risoni into the broth and simmer for 12 minutes, or until *al dente*.

Return the chicken to the broth along with the spinach and dill. Simmer for 2 minutes, or until the spinach has wilted. Stir in the lemon juice, season to taste with salt and freshly ground black pepper and serve.

Serves 4

Beef in black bean sauce

4 tablespoons canned salted black
  beans in soy sauce
750 g rump steak
1 tablespoon peanut oil
1 tablespoon sesame oil
1 large onion, thinly sliced
1 clove garlic, finely chopped
4 cm x 1 cm piece of fresh ginger,
  peeled and finely chopped
1 small fresh red chilli, finely chopped
2 teaspoons cornflour
2 tablespoons dark soy sauce
1 teaspoon sugar
1/4 cup (60 ml) beef stock
1 spring onion, thinly sliced on the
  diagonal, to garnish

Rinse and then soak the black beans
in cold water for 5 minutes. Drain and
roughly mash the beans with a fork.
Trim the steak of all fat and sinew,
then cut the meat in thin slices across
the grain.

Heat a saucepan over medium heat,
add half each of the peanut and
sesame oils. Add the beef in two
batches, and stir each for 2 minutes,
or until well browned. Transfer the
beef and any liquid to a bowl. Heat
the remaining oils, add the onion and
stir for 2 minutes. Add the garlic,
ginger and chilli, and stir for 1 minute.

Mix the cornflour with 1 teaspoon
water, then return the beef and any
cooking liquid to the pan with the
black beans, soy sauce, sugar,
stock and cornflour paste. Stir for
1–2 minutes, or until the sauce boils
and thickens. Garnish with the spring
onions and serve with steamed rice.

Serves 4

Spaghetti Niçoise

350 g spaghetti
8 quail eggs (or 4 hen eggs)
3 x 185 g cans tuna in oil
⅓ cup (50 g) pitted and halved
  Kalamata olives
100 g semi-dried tomatoes,
  halved lengthways
4 anchovy fillets, chopped into
  small pieces
1 teaspoon finely grated lemon rind
2 tablespoons lemon juice
3 tablespoons baby capers, drained
3 tablespoons chopped fresh
  flat-leaf parsley

Cook the pasta in a large saucepan of rapidly boiling salted water until *al dente*. Meanwhile, place the eggs in a saucepan of cold water, bring to the boil and cook for 4 minutes (10 minutes for hen eggs). Drain, cool under cold water, then peel. Cut the quail eggs into halves or the hen eggs into quarters.

Empty the tuna and its oil into a large bowl. Add the olives, tomato halves, anchovies, lemon rind and juice, capers and 2 tablespoons of the parsley. Drain the pasta and rinse in a little cold water, then toss gently through the tuna mixture. Divide among serving bowls, garnish with egg and the remaining chopped fresh parsley, and serve.

Serves 4–6

Penne with pumpkin, baked ricotta and prosciutto

500 g penne
460 g butternut pumpkin,
  cut into 1 cm cubes
¼ cup (60 ml) extra virgin olive oil
2 cloves garlic, crushed
100 g semi-dried tomatoes, chopped
4 slices prosciutto, chopped
250 g baked ricotta, cut into
  1 cm cubes
3 tablespoons shredded fresh basil

Cook the penne in a large saucepan of rapidly boiling salted water until *al dente*. Drain. Meanwhile, cook the pumpkin in a saucepan of boiling water for 10–12 minutes, or until just tender, then drain.

Heat the oil in a large saucepan, add the garlic and cook over medium heat for 30 seconds. Add the tomato, prosciutto, pumpkin and penne and toss gently over low heat for 1–2 minutes, or until heated through.

Add the baked ricotta and the basil, season with salt and cracked black pepper and serve immediately.

Serves 4

Chicken, artichoke and broad bean stew

1 cup (155 g) frozen broad beans
8 chicken thighs on the bone
  (skin removed, optional)
½ cup (60 g) seasoned plain flour
2 tablespoons oil
1 large red onion, cut into small
  wedges
½ cup (125 ml) dry white wine
1¼ cups (310 ml) chicken stock
2 teaspoons finely chopped fresh
  rosemary
340 g marinated artichokes,
  well drained and quartered
800 g potatoes, cut into large pieces
60 g butter

Remove the skins from the broad beans. Coat the chicken in the flour, shaking off the excess. Heat the oil in a saucepan or flameproof casserole dish, then brown the chicken in two batches on all sides over medium heat. Remove and drain on crumpled paper towels.

Add the onion to the pan and cook for 3–4 minutes, or until soft but not brown. Increase the heat to high, pour in the wine and boil for 2 minutes, or until reduced to a syrup. Stir in 1 cup (250 ml) stock and bring just to the boil, then return the chicken to the saucepan with the rosemary. Reduce the heat to low and simmer, covered, for 45 minutes. Add the artichokes, increase the heat to high and return to the boil. Reduce to a simmer and cook, uncovered, for 10–15 minutes. Add the beans and cook for 5 minutes.

Meanwhile, cook the potato in a saucepan of boiling water for 15–20 minutes, or until tender. Drain, then return to the pan. Add the butter and the remaining stock and mash with a potato masher. Serve on the side of the stew.

Serves 4

Note: Although this dish takes a while to cook, it is prepared very quickly.

Freeform ricotta and mushroom lasagne

1 cup (250 g) fresh ricotta
2/3 cup (65 g) grated Parmesan
3 1/2 tablespoons olive oil
1 onion, thinly sliced
2 cloves garlic, crushed
500 g Swiss brown mushrooms, sliced
300 ml good-quality Italian tomato pasta sauce
6 sheets fresh lasagne, cut in half, then cut into 12 cm squares
200 g baby spinach leaves, washed

Mix the ricotta with half the Parmesan and season well. Heat 2 tablespoons oil in a large frying pan, add the onion and cook for 2 minutes, or until it softens. Add the garlic and mushrooms and cook for 1–2 minutes, or until the mushrooms start to soften. Add the tomato pasta sauce and cook for another 5–6 minutes, or until the sauce starts to thicken. Season well.

Meanwhile, bring a deep saucepan of water to a boil, add 1 tablespoon oil and a pinch of salt. Cook the lasagne squares and cook for 2–3 minutes, or until cooked. Drain, keeping each square separate. Put the spinach in a pan with just the water clinging to the leaves. Cover and cook over medium heat for 1–2 minutes, or until the spinach has wilted.

To assemble, place a pasta square on each serving plate, then divide the mushroom sauce among the squares. Place another pasta square on top, then spread the ricotta mixture evenly over the surface, leaving a 2 cm border. Divide the spinach evenly among the four servings. Finally, place another pasta square on top, brush or drizzle with the remaining oil, then sprinkle with the remaining Parmesan. Season. Serve with a green salad and crusty bread.

Serves 4

Moroccan chicken

1 tablespoon Moroccan spice blend
800 g chicken thigh fillets, trimmed
  and halved
1 tablespoon oil
60 g butter
1 large onion, cut into wedges
1 cinnamon stick
2 cloves garlic, crushed
2 tablespoons lemon juice
1 cup (250 ml) chicken stock
⅓ cup (75 g) pitted prunes, halved
1½ cups (225 g) couscous
lemon wedges, for serving

Sprinkle half the spice blend over the chicken. Heat the oil and 20 g of the butter in a large saucepan or deep-sided frying pan over medium heat. Cook the chicken in two batches for 5 minutes, or until evenly browned. Remove from the pan, then add the onion and cinnamon stick and cook for 2–3 minutes before adding the garlic. Return the chicken to the pan and add the lemon juice and the remaining spice blend. Season, then cook, covered, for 5 minutes.

Add the stock and prunes to the pan and bring to the boil. Reduce the heat to medium–low and cook, uncovered, for 15 minutes, or until the chicken is cooked and the liquid has reduced to a sauce. Before serving, stir 20 g of the butter into the sauce.

About 10 minutes before the chicken is ready, place the couscous in a heatproof bowl, add 1½ cups (375 ml) boiling water, and stand for 3–5 minutes. Stir in the remaining butter and fluff with a fork until the butter has melted and the grains separate. Serve with the chicken.

Serves 4

Tagliatelle with feta, tomato and rocket

4 vine-ripened tomatoes
1 small red onion, finely chopped
4 tablespoons shredded fresh basil
2 tablespoons olive oil
375 g tagliatelle
2 cloves garlic, finely chopped
150 g baby rocket leaves
150 g soft feta, crumbled
1/4 cup (15 g) fresh small whole basil
  leaves

Score a cross in the base of each tomato, then place in a bowl of boiling water for 1 minute. Plunge into cold water and peel the skin away from the cross. Cut in half and remove the seeds with a teaspoon. Chop, then transfer to a bowl. Add the onion and basil, stir in 1 tablespoon of the oil and set aside.

Cook the pasta in a large saucepan of rapidly boiling salted water until *al dente*. Drain, reserving 1/2 cup (125 ml) of the water. Return the pasta to the pan, add the remaining oil, the garlic and the reserved pasta water and toss together over medium heat for 1–2 minutes to warm through. Stir in the tomato mixture, rocket and feta. Season to taste with salt and pepper. Divide among four serving plates and serve immediately, garnished with the whole basil leaves.

Serves 4

Pasta with beef ragù

100 g streaky bacon or pancetta
(not trimmed), finely chopped
1 onion, finely chopped
3 cloves garlic, crushed
1 bay leaf
800 g lean beef mince
2 cups (500 ml) red wine
⅓ cup (90 g) tomato paste
(tomato purée)
400 g tagliatelle
freshly grated Parmesan, to garnish

Heat a large deep frying pan (preferably stainless steel or non-coated). Add the bacon or pancetta and cook over medium–high heat for 2 minutes, or until soft and just starting to brown. Add the onion, garlic and bay leaf and cook for 2 minutes, or until the onion is soft and just starting to brown.

Add the mince and stir for about 4 minutes, or until the mince browns, breaking up any lumps with the back of a wooden spoon. Add the wine, tomato paste and 1 cup (250 ml) water and stir well. Bring to the boil, then reduce the heat and simmer, covered, for 40 minutes. Remove the lid and cook for another 40 minutes, or until reduced to a thick, glossy sauce.

About 20 minutes before the ragù is ready, bring a large saucepan of salted water to a rapid boil and cook the pasta until *al dente*. Drain. Serve the sauce over the pasta and garnish with a little grated Parmesan.

Serves 4

Note: This recipe is ready to cook in no time but it takes a while to simmer.

Spaghetti bolognese

1 tablespoon olive oil
1 large onion, diced
2 cloves garlic, crushed
600 g beef mince
½ cup (125 g) red wine
½ cup (125 g) beef stock
2 x 400 g cans chopped tomatoes
1 carrot, grated
350 g spaghetti

Heat the oil over medium heat in a large saucepan, add the onion and garlic and cook for 1–2 minutes, or until soft. Add the mince and cook, stirring to break up any lumps, for 5 minutes, or until the meat is browned. Pour in the wine and simmer for 2–3 minutes, or until reduced slightly, then add the stock and simmer for another 2 minutes. Add the tomato and carrot and season well with salt and pepper. Cook over low heat for 40 minutes.

About 15 minutes before serving time, cook the pasta in a large saucepan of rapidly boiling salted water until al dente. Drain well and keep warm. Divide the pasta among four serving bowls and pour the meat sauce over the pasta. Garnish with parsley, if desired.

Serves 4

Note: This dish cooks for a long time but doesn't take long to prepare.

Coconut beef curry on turmeric rice

2 tablespoons oil
1 large onion, sliced
2 tablespoons vindaloo curry paste
1 kg chuck steak, trimmed and cubed
1 cup (250 ml) beef stock
200 ml coconut cream
1 1/4 cups (250 g) basmati rice
3/4 teaspoon ground turmeric

Heat the oil in a large saucepan over medium–high heat. Add the onion and cook for 2–3 minutes, or until starting to soften. Add the curry paste and stir for 1 minute, or until fragrant. Add the steak and brown evenly for about 5 minutes.

Pour in the stock and bring to the boil. Reduce the heat to very low and simmer, covered, for 1 hour, or until the meat is tender. Uncover and cook for 15 minutes to reduce the sauce.

Add the coconut cream, return to the boil, then simmer over low heat for 15–20 minutes, or until the beef is tender and the sauce has reduced.

About 25 minutes before the beef is ready, rinse the rice and place it in a large saucepan. Add the turmeric and 1 3/4 cups (440 ml) water and bring to the boil. Reduce the heat to very low, then cook, covered, for 10 minutes. Remove from the heat and leave to stand, covered, for 10 minutes. Divide the rice among four wide serving bowls and top with the beef curry.

Serves 4

Note: Although this curry cooks for a long time, it is prepared very quickly.

Pot

Chicken and cider stew with apple and potato mash

1 kg chicken thigh fillets, trimmed and cut into 2 cm cubes
1½ tablespoons finely chopped fresh thyme
1 tablespoon oil
90 g butter
3 French shallots, thinly sliced
1½ cups (375 ml) apple cider
1 kg potatoes, cubed
2 large green apples, peeled, cored and sliced into eighths
2/3 cup (170 ml) cream

Season the chicken with 2 teaspoons of the thyme and salt and black pepper. Heat the oil and 20 g of the butter in a large saucepan over medium heat. Brown the chicken in two batches for 2–3 minutes. Remove.

Add the French shallots and the remaining thyme to the pan and sauté for 2 minutes. Pour in the cider, then bring to the boil, scraping off any sediment from the bottom. Return the chicken to the pan and cover. Reduce the heat to medium–low and cook for 35–40 minutes, or until the chicken is tender and the sauce has reduced (check occasionally to see if any water needs to be added).

Meanwhile, cook the potato and apple in a saucepan of boiling water for 15–20 minutes, or until tender. Drain and return to the pan over low heat for a minute to allow any water to evaporate. Remove from the heat, and mash with a potato masher. Stir in 2 tablespoons of the cream and the remaining butter with a wooden spoon, then season well with salt and pepper.

Stir the remaining cream into the stew and cook for another 2–4 minutes, or until the sauce has thickened. Serve at once with the potato and apple mash and a crisp green salad.

Serves 4

Vegetable tagine with couscous

¼ cup (60 ml) olive oil
1 large red capsicum (pepper),
  seeded and cut into quarters
1 large eggplant (aubergine), sliced
  into 1 cm rounds, then in half again
400 g can chopped tomatoes
1 tablespoon harissa paste (see Note)
1 tablespoon Moroccan spice blend
1 cup (250 ml) vegetable stock
2 large zucchini, cut into 2 cm chunks
1½ cups (225 g) couscous
20 g butter

Heat 1 tablespoon of the oil in a saucepan over medium–high heat. Sauté the capsicum, skin-side-down, covered, for 3–4 minutes, or until the skin is well browned. Remove from the pan. Peel, then cut the flesh into 1 cm slices. Heat the remaining oil in the pan and cook the eggplant in batches over medium–high heat for 4–5 minutes, or until well browned.

Return the capsicum to the pan, then stir in the tomato, harissa paste and Moroccan spice blend. Pour in the stock and bring to the boil. Reduce the heat to medium–low and simmer, uncovered, for 15 minutes. Add the zucchini and eggplant and cook for another 8 minutes, or until the vegetables are tender.

About 10 minutes before the vegetables are ready, place the couscous in a heatproof bowl, add 1½ cups (375 ml) boiling water, and leave for 3–5 minutes. Stir in the butter and fluff with a fork until the butter has melted and the grains separate. Serve the vegetable tagine with the couscous.

Serves 4

Note: Harissa is a blend of chillies, garlic, spices and oil available at specialist food stores.

Tomato and basil black mussels

½ cup (125 ml) dry white wine
2 bay leaves
1 kg black mussels, scrubbed and
  beards removed
2 cups (500 g) tomato pasta sauce
1–2 teaspoons sugar, to taste
2 tablespoons extra virgin olive oil
4 tablespoons shredded fresh basil
2 tablespoons snipped fresh chives

Place the wine and bay leaves in a large wide saucepan and bring to the boil. Discard any broken mussels, add the rest to the saucepan and cook, covered with a tight-fitting lid, over high heat for 4 minutes, or until the mussels open.

Place the pasta sauce, sugar, oil and basil in a bowl, and mix together well.

Discard any mussels which have not opened. Drain, reserving the cooking juices. Return the mussels to the saucepan, add the tomato mixture and ½ cup (125 ml) of the reserved cooking juices, and stir over high heat for 3–4 minutes, or until warmed through. Sprinkle with chives and serve in warmed bowls with bread.

Serves 4

Fresh vegetable lasagne with rocket

Balsamic syrup
1/3 cup (80 ml) balsamic vinegar
1 1/2 tablespoons brown sugar

16 asparagus spears, trimmed and
  cut into 5 cm lengths
1 cup (150 g) fresh or frozen peas
2 large zucchini (courgettes), cut into
  thin ribbons
2 fresh lasagne sheets (200 g),
  (each sheet 24 cm x 35 cm)
100 g rocket leaves
1 cup (30 g) fresh basil, torn
2 tablespoons extra virgin olive oil
250 g low-fat ricotta
150 g semi-dried tomatoes
Parmesan shavings, to garnish

Stir the vinegar and brown sugar in a small saucepan over medium heat until the sugar dissolves. Reduce the heat and simmer for 3–4 minutes, or until the sauce becomes syrupy. Remove from the heat.

Bring a large saucepan of salted water to the boil. Blanch the asparagus, peas and zucchini in separate batches until just tender, refreshing each batch in cold water. Return the cooking liquid to the boil. Cook the lasagne sheets in the boiling water for 1–2 minutes, or until *al dente*. Refresh in cold water and drain well. Cut each sheet in half lengthways.

Toss the vegetables and the rocket with the basil and olive oil. Season. To assemble, place one strip of pasta on a serving plate—one-third on the centre of the plate and two-thirds overhanging one side. Place a small amount of the salad on the centre one third, topped with some ricotta and tomato. Season lightly and fold over one-third of the lasagne sheet. Top with a layer of salad, ricotta and tomato. Fold back the final layer of pasta and garnish with salad and tomato. Repeat with the remaining pasta, salad, ricotta and tomato to make four. Drizzle with the balsamic syrup and garnish with Parmesan.

Serves 4

Farfalle with spinach and bacon

400 g farfalle
2 tablespoons extra virgin olive oil
250 g bacon, chopped
1 red onion, finely chopped
250 g baby English spinach leaves, stalks trimmed
1–2 tablespoons sweet chilli sauce (optional)
¼ cup (35 g) crumbled goat's feta

Cook the pasta in a large saucepan of rapidly boiling salted water until al dente, then drain and return to the saucepan. Meanwhile, heat the oil in a frying pan, add the bacon and cook over medium heat for 3 minutes, or until golden. Add the onion and cook for another 4 minutes, or until softened. Toss the spinach leaves through the onion and bacon mixture for 30 seconds, or until just wilted.

Add the bacon and spinach mixture to the drained pasta, then stir in the sweet chilli sauce. Season to taste with salt and cracked black pepper and toss well. Spoon into warm bowls and scatter with the crumbled feta. Serve immediately.

Serves 4

Madras lamb pilau

¼ cup (60 ml) oil
2 onions, thinly sliced
1 cup (250 g) plain yoghurt
¼ cup (60 g) Madras curry paste
2 cups (400 g) basmati rice, well
  rinsed
8 large French-trimmed lamb cutlets
4 tablespoons chopped fresh mint
½ cup (60 g) slivered almonds,
  lightly toasted

Heat 2 tablespoons of the oil in a large saucepan, add the onions and cook over medium heat for 4–5 minutes, or until soft. Remove half with a slotted spoon, set aside and keep warm. Add 200 g of the yoghurt and 2 tablespoons of the curry paste to the pan. Cook, stirring, for 2 minutes. Stir in the rice until well coated. Pour in 2 cups (500 ml) water, bring to the boil, then reduce the heat to medium–low and cook for 15–20 minutes, or until all the water has been absorbed and the rice is tender.

Meanwhile, smear the cutlets with the remaining curry paste and marinate for 5 minutes. Heat the remaining oil in a frying pan over high heat, then cook the cutlets for 3–4 minutes on each side, or until cooked to your liking. Remove from the heat, cover with foil and allow to rest. Combine the remaining yoghurt with 1 tablespoon of the mint.

To serve, stir the remaining mint through the rice, season, then divide among four serving plates. Top with the remaining onions, the lamb and the almonds. Serve with a dollop of the minted yoghurt on the side.

Serves 4

Pan

Fillet steak with mixed mushrooms and sherry

250 g broccoli, cut into large florets
250 g green beans, topped and tailed
1 tablespoon oil
60 g butter
4 rib eye steaks (scotch fillet) (about
   160 g each), 2.5 cm thick
3 cloves garlic, finely chopped
250 g mixed mushrooms (portabella,
   Swiss brown, shiitake or button)
2 teaspoons chopped fresh thyme
½ cup (125 ml) dry sherry

Bring a saucepan of lightly salted water to the boil. Add the broccoli and beans and cook for 3–4 minutes, or until tender but still crisp. Drain.

Melt the oil and 20 g of the butter in a large stainless steel frying pan. Cook the steaks for 3–4 minutes on each side for medium–rare, or until cooked to your liking. Remove from the pan, cover with foil and rest.

Melt another 20 g of the butter in the pan over medium heat. Add the garlic and mushrooms and season to taste. Cook for 3–4 minutes, or until the mushrooms have softened. Stir in the thyme. Remove from the pan.

Add the sherry and any juices from the rested meat to the pan and stir to scrape up any sediment from the base. Bring to the boil, then reduce the heat and simmer for 2–3 minutes, or until reduced to ⅓ cup (80 ml) and thickened slightly. Whisk in the remaining butter in small amounts, until glossy.

To serve, put the steaks on four serving plates, top with the mushrooms and spoon the sauce over the top. Serve with the broccoli and green beans.

Serves 4

Deep-fried calamari in chickpea batter with parsley salad

Deep-fried calamari
150 g besan (chickpea flour)
1½ teaspoons smoked paprika
  or paprika
1½ teaspoons ground cumin
½ teaspoon baking powder
1 cup (250 ml) soda water
oil, for deep-frying
6 cleaned squid hoods, cut into rings
  about 8 mm wide

Parsley salad
¼ preserved lemon, rinsed, pith
  and flesh removed
¼ cup (60 ml) lemon juice
¼ cup (60 ml) extra virgin olive oil
1 clove garlic, finely chopped
1 cup (20 g) fresh flat-leaf parsley
harissa, to serve (optional)

To make the batter, sift the besan, paprika, cumin and baking powder into a bowl, add ¼ teaspoon pepper, mix together and make a well in the centre. Gradually add the soda water, whisking until smooth. Season with salt. Cover, then leave for 30 minutes.

Cut the lemon rind into very thin slivers. To make the dressing, whisk the lemon juice, extra virgin olive oil and garlic together in a bowl.

Fill a large heavy-based saucepan or wok one-third full of oil and heat until a cube of bread dropped into the oil browns in 15 seconds.

Dip the calamari into the batter, allowing any excess to drip away. Cook in batches for 30–60 seconds, or until pale gold and crisp all over. Drain well on crumpled paper towels and keep warm.

Add the parsley and lemon slivers to the dressing, tossing to coat the leaves. Divide the leaves among four bowls or plates. Top with the calamari rings and serve with harissa.

Serves 4 as an entrée

Sesame-coated tuna with coriander salsa

4 tuna steaks
3/4 cup (115 g) sesame seeds
100 g baby rocket leaves

Coriander salsa
2 tomatoes, seeded and diced
1 large clove garlic, crushed
2 tablespoons finely chopped
   fresh coriander leaves
2 tablespoons virgin olive oil,
   plus extra for shallow-frying
1 tablespoon lime juice

Cut each tuna steak into 3 pieces. Place the sesame seeds on a sheet of baking paper. Roll the tuna in the sesame seeds to coat. Refrigerate for 15 minutes.

To make the salsa, place the tomato, garlic, coriander, oil and lime juice in a bowl, and mix together well. Cover and refrigerate until ready to use.

Fill a heavy-based frying pan to 1.5 cm with the extra oil and place over high heat. Add the tuna in two batches and cook for 2 minutes each side (it should be pink in the centre). Remove and drain on paper towels. To serve, divide the rocket among four serving plates and arrange the tuna over the top. Spoon the salsa on the side and serve immediately. Top with a teaspoon of chilli jam, if desired, and season.

Serves 4

Veal scaloppine with white wine and parsley

4 x 170 g veal escalopes
30 g butter
¼ cup (60 ml) dry white wine
  or dry Marsala (not sweet)
100 ml thick (double) cream
1 tablespoon wholegrain mustard
2 tablespoons chopped fresh
  flat-leaf parsley

Place the veal escalopes between two sheets of plastic wrap and either press down hard with the heel of your hand until flattened, or flatten with a rolling pin or mallet. Heat the butter in a frying pan and cook the escalopes in batches for 1 minute each side, or until just cooked. Remove and cover.

Add the wine to the pan, bring to the boil and cook for 1–2 minutes, or until reduced by half. Then add the cream, bring to the boil and reduce by half again. Stir in the mustard and 1 tablespoon parsley until just combined. Return the veal to the pan to warm through and coat in the sauce. Serve the veal with a little sauce and sprinkle with the remaining parsley. Serve with potatoes and a green salad, if desired.

Serves 4

Salt and pepper chicken with Asian greens and oyster sauce

1¼ cups (250 g) jasmine rice
⅓ cup (40 g) plain flour
¾ teaspoon five-spice powder
1½ teaspoons sea salt
1 teaspoon ground white pepper
750 g chicken breast fillets, cut into
   thin strips (1 cm x 5 cm)
145 ml peanut oil
1.25 kg mixed Asian greens (bok
   choy, choy sum or gai larn)
½ cup (125 ml) oyster sauce

Bring a large saucepan of water to the boil. Add the rice and cook for 12 minutes, stirring occasionally. Drain well.

Meanwhile, combine the flour, five-spice powder, salt and pepper in a large bowl. Toss the chicken strips in the flour until well coated. Heat ¼ cup (60 ml) of the oil in a large frying pan over medium–high heat. Add the chicken in three batches and cook, turning, for about 3 minutes, or until browned. Drain on crumpled paper towels and keep warm.

Heat the remaining oil and cook the mixed Asian greens over medium–high heat for 1–2 minutes. Add the oyster sauce and toss through. Serve on a bed of jasmine rice topped with the chicken strips.

Serves 4

Lamb backstraps with spiced lentils and mint raita

½ cup (125 g) plain yoghurt
2 tablespoons finely chopped
  fresh mint
1 tablespoon garam masala
3 teaspoons ground cumin
½ teaspoon chilli powder
⅓ cup (80 ml) oil
4 lamb backstraps or eye of loin fillets
  (about 150 g each)
2 teaspoons grated fresh ginger
1 teaspoon ground turmeric
2 x 425 g cans lentils, drained
  and rinsed

Combine the yoghurt and half the mint in a small non-metallic bowl. Cover and set aside.

Dry-fry the garam masala in a frying pan over medium heat for 1 minute, or until fragrant. Remove, then dry-fry the cumin. Combine 2 teaspoons each of garam masala and cumin, the chilli and 2 tablespoons oil. Put the lamb in a non-metallic dish. Brush with the spiced oil, cover and marinate for 10 minutes, or overnight, if possible.

Meanwhile, heat 1 tablespoon of the remaining oil in a saucepan. Add the ginger, turmeric and remaining cumin and cook for 30 seconds, or until fragrant. Add the lentils and stir until heated through. Reduce the heat to low, add the remaining garam masala and season with salt. Cover and cook for 5 minutes, adding ¼ cup (60 ml) water if the lentils start to stick. Before serving, stir in the remaining mint.

Heat a large frying pan over medium–high heat and add the remaining oil. Cook the backstraps for 3–4 minutes each side for medium–rare, or until cooked to your liking. Leave for several minutes, then cut into 1 cm slices. Place some lentils on a plate, arrange the lamb slices on top and serve with mint raita.

Serves 4

Swordfish with tomato salsa and garlic mash

500 g potatoes, cubed
2 large vine-ripened tomatoes
2 tablespoons finely shredded
    fresh basil
1 tablespoon balsamic vinegar
3 cloves garlic, finely chopped
145 ml olive oil
4 swordfish steaks
    (about 200 g each)

Cook the potato in a large saucepan of boiling water for 12–15 minutes, or until tender.

To make the salsa, score a cross in the base of each tomato. Place in a heatproof bowl and cover with boiling water. Leave for 30 seconds, then plunge into iced water and peel away from the cross. Cut the tomatoes in half, scoop out the seeds and discard. Finely dice the flesh, then combine with the basil, vinegar, 2 cloves garlic and 2 tablespoons oil. Season.

Heat ¼ cup (60 ml) of the olive oil in a large non-stick frying pan over medium–high heat. Season the swordfish well, then add to the frying pan and cook for 2–3 minutes on each side for medium–rare, or until cooked to your liking.

Just before the swordfish is ready, drain the potato. Add the remaining olive oil and garlic, and season to taste. Mash until smooth with a potato masher.

To serve, put the swordfish steaks on four serving plates and top with the tomato salsa. Serve the garlic mash on the side.

Serves 4

Pork with paprika, potatoes and shallots

1 tablespoon paprika
4 thick pork loin cutlets
2 tablespoons olive oil
¼ cup (60 ml) sherry vinegar
¼ teaspoon cayenne pepper
½ cup (125 ml) puréed tomato
400 g potatoes, cut into 2 cm cubes
8 French shallots, peeled
200 g rocket leaves

Combine the paprika with ¼ teaspoon each of salt and freshly ground black pepper. Sprinkle over both sides of the pork. Heat the oil over medium heat in a deep frying pan large enough to fit the cutlets in a single layer. Cook the cutlets until brown on both sides.

Pour the sherry vinegar into the pan and stir well to scrape up any sediment stuck to the base. Stir in the cayenne pepper, puréed tomato and 1 cup (250 ml) hot water. Bring to the boil, then add the potato and shallots. Reduce the heat, cover and simmer for 30 minutes, or until the sauce has thickened and reduced by half—check the liquid level once or twice, and add a little water if necessary. Season.

To serve, divide the rocket leaves among four serving plates and place a cutlet on top. Spoon the sauce and potatoes over the top.

Serves 4

Salt and pepper squid

1 cup (125 g) cornflour
1½ tablespoons salt
1 tablespoon ground white pepper
3 small fresh red chillies,
  seeded, chopped
1 kg cleaned squid tubes, sliced
  into rings
2 egg whites, lightly beaten
oil, for deep-frying
lime wedges, for serving

Combine the cornflour, salt, pepper and chilli in a bowl.

Dip the squid rings into the egg white and then into the cornflour mixture. Shake off any excess cornflour.

Fill a deep, heavy-based saucepan one third full of oil and heat to 180°C (350°F), or until a cube of bread dropped into the oil browns in 15 seconds. Cook the squid in batches for 1–2 minutes, or until lightly golden all over. Drain on crumpled paper towels. Serve hot with steamed rice and lime wedges.

Serves 4

Japanese-style steak salad

750 g rump steak
3 teaspoons oil
3 teaspoons wasabi paste
½ teaspoon Dijon mustard
1 teaspoon grated fresh ginger
2 tablespoons rice wine vinegar
3 tablespoons pickled ginger, plus
   1 tablespoon pickling liquid
2 tablespoons sesame oil
¼ cup (60 ml) oil, extra
100 g baby spinach leaves
100 g mizuna or watercress, trimmed
4 radishes, thinly sliced
1 Lebanese cucumber, peeled and
   cut into ribbons with a vegetable
   peeler
¼ cup (40 g) sesame seeds, toasted

Generously season the steak with salt and freshly cracked black pepper. Heat the oil in a large frying pan or heat a barbecue plate to very hot. Add the steak and cook for 2–3 minutes on each side, or until browned. Remove and leave to rest, covered, for 5 minutes.

Put the wasabi paste, mustard, ginger, rice wine vinegar, pickled ginger, pickling liquid and ½ teaspoon salt in a large bowl and whisk together. Whisk in the oils, then add the spinach, mizuna, radish and cucumber to the bowl and toss well.

Slice the steak across the grain into thin strips. Divide the salad among four serving plates, top with the beef slices and sprinkle with sesame seeds. Serve immediately.

Serves 4

Stuffed chicken breast with tomato, goat's cheese and asparagus

4 large chicken breast fillets
100 g semi-dried tomatoes
100 g goat's cheese, sliced
200 g asparagus spears, trimmed,
  halved and blanched
50 g butter
1½ cups (375 ml) chicken stock
2 zucchini (courgettes), cut into
  5 cm batons
1 cup (250 ml) cream
8 spring onions, thinly sliced

Pound each chicken breast between two sheets of plastic wrap with a mallet or rolling pin until 1 cm thick. Divide the tomato, goat's cheese and 155 g of the asparagus pieces among the breasts. Roll up tightly lengthways, securing along the seam with toothpicks.

Heat the butter in a large frying pan over medium heat. Add the chicken, then brown on all sides. Pour in the stock, then reduce the heat to low. Cook, covered, for 10 minutes, or until the chicken is cooked through. Remove the chicken and keep warm.

Meanwhile, bring a saucepan of lightly salted water to the boil. Add the zucchini and remaining asparagus and cook for 2 minutes, or until just tender. Remove from the pan. Whisk the cream into the frying pan. Add the spring onion and simmer over medium–low heat for 4 minutes, or until reduced and thickened. To serve, cut each chicken roll in half on the diagonal and place on serving plates. Spoon on the sauce and serve with the greens.

Serves 4

Beer-battered fish fillets with chips

¼ cup (30 g) self-raising flour
¼ cup (30 g) cornflour
1 cup (125 g) plain flour
1 cup (250 ml) beer
(use any type to vary the flavour)
oil, for deep-frying
4 large pontiac potatoes, cut into finger-size chips
4 flathead fillets (about 200 g each), or other white fish fillets (snapper, blue eye or John Dory), skinned and pin-boned
2 lemons, cut into wedges

Preheat the oven to moderate 180°C (350°F/Gas 4). Sift the self-raising flour, cornflour and ½ cup (60 g) of the plain flour into a large bowl and make a well. Gradually whisk in the beer to make a smooth batter. Cover.

Fill a large heavy-based saucepan one-third full of oil and heat to 180°C (350°F), or until a cube of bread dropped into the oil browns in 15 seconds. Deep-fry batches of potato chips for 2–4 minutes, or until pale golden. Drain on paper towels. Deep-fry again for 3 minutes, or until golden and cooked through. Keep hot in the oven while you cook the fish.

Reheat the oil to 180°C (350°F). Stir the batter, then coat the fish fillets in the remaining plain flour, shaking off the excess. Dip the fillets into the batter, allowing the excess to drip off a little. Slowly ease the fillets into the hot oil, holding the tail out for a few seconds—turn with tongs if necessary. Cook for 4–5 minutes, or until golden brown and the fish is cooked through. Remove with a slotted spoon and drain on crumpled paper towels. Serve with the chips, lemon wedges and a green salad.

Serves 4

Nori omelette with stir-fried vegetables

8 eggs
18 cm x 10 cm sheet nori
¼ cup (60 ml) oil
1 clove garlic, crushed
3 teaspoons finely grated fresh ginger
1 carrot, cut into thick matchsticks
2 zucchini (courgettes), halved
   lengthways, sliced on the diagonal
200 g mix of Swiss brown, enoki
   and oyster mushrooms,
   larger ones sliced
1 tablespoon Japanese soy sauce
1 tablespoon mirin
2 teaspoons yellow miso paste

Lightly beat the eggs. Roll the nori up tightly and snip with scissors into very fine strips. Add to the eggs and season to taste with salt and cracked black pepper.

Heat a wok over high heat, add 2 teaspoons of the oil and swirl to coat the side of the wok. Add ⅓ cup (80 ml) of the egg mixture and swirl to coat the base of the wok. Cook for 2 minutes, or until set, then turn over and cook the other side for 1 minute. Remove and keep warm. Repeat with the remaining mixture, adding another 2 teaspoons of the oil each time, to make four omelettes.

Heat the remaining oil in the wok, add the garlic and ginger and stir-fry for 1 minute. Add the carrot, zucchini and mushrooms in two batches and stir-fry for 3 minutes, or until softened. Return all the vegetables to the wok. Add the soy sauce, mirin and miso paste, and simmer for 1 minute. Divide the vegetables evenly among the omelettes, roll them up and serve immediately with steamed rice.

Serves 4

Teriyaki chicken with ginger chive rice

4 small chicken breast fillets, skin on
  (about 170 g each)
¼ cup (60 ml) Japanese soy sauce
2 tablespoons sake
1½ tablespoons mirin
1½ tablespoons soft brown sugar
3 teaspoons finely grated fresh ginger
1½ cups (300 g) long-grain rice
2 tablespoons finely chopped
  fresh chives
2 tablespoons oil

Pound each breast between sheets of plastic wrap with a mallet until 1 cm thick. Put the soy sauce, sake, mirin, sugar and 1 teaspoon ginger in a flat non-metallic dish and stir until the sugar has dissolved. Add the chicken and turn to coat. Cover and refrigerate for 1 hour, turning once halfway through.

Bring a large saucepan of water to the boil. Add the rice and cook for 12 minutes, stirring occasionally. Drain. Stir in the chives and remaining ginger, then cover until ready to serve.

Drain the chicken, reserving the marinade. Heat the oil in a deep frying pan and cook the chicken, skin-side-down over medium heat for 5 minutes, until the skin is crisp. Turn and cook for 4 minutes (not quite cooked).

Add the marinade and ¼ cup (60 ml) water to the pan and scrape up any sediment. Bring to the boil over high heat, then add the chicken (skin-side-up) and juices. Cook for 5–6 minutes, until cooked through, turning once. (If the sauce is runny, remove the chicken and boil the sauce until syrupy.) Serve the chicken whole or sliced, drizzled with the sauce.

Serves 4

Salmon and dill potato patties with lime mayonnaise

400 g new potatoes, cut in half
2 teaspoons grated lime rind
1¼ cups (310 g) whole-egg
  mayonnaise
425 g can salmon, drained,
  bones removed
1 tablespoon chopped fresh dill
2 spring onions, thinly sliced
1 egg
1 cup (80 g) fresh breadcrumbs
¼ cup (60 ml) oil
200 g rocket leaves
lime wedges, to serve

Cook the potatoes in a large saucepan of boiling water for 12–15 minutes, or until tender. Drain well and cool.

Meanwhile, combine the lime rind and 1 cup (250 g) of the mayonnaise.

Transfer the potato to a large bowl, then mash roughly with the back of a spoon, leaving some large chunks. Stir in the salmon, dill and spring onion and season. Mix in the egg and the remaining mayonnaise. Divide into eight portions, forming palm-size patties. Press lightly into the breadcrumbs to coat.

Heat the oil in a non-stick frying pan and cook the patties, turning, for 3–4 minutes, or until golden brown. Drain on paper towels. Serve with a dollop of lime mayonnaise, rocket leaves and lime wedges.

Serves 4

Spice-crusted salmon and noodle salad

½ teaspoon wasabi paste
⅓ cup (80 ml) Japanese soy sauce
5 tablespoons mirin
1 teaspoon sugar
250 g dried somen noodles
1 teaspoon sesame oil
1 teaspoon sansho powder
1 tablespoon vegetable oil
3 salmon fillets (about 200 g each),
    skin removed
4 spring onions, finely sliced
    on the diagonal
½ cup (15 g) fresh coriander leaves
1 Lebanese cucumber, halved
    lengthways, thinly sliced

Combine the wasabi with a little of the Japanese soy sauce to form a smooth paste. Stir in the mirin, sugar and remaining soy sauce.

Cook the noodles in a large saucepan of boiling salted water for 2 minutes, or until tender. Drain and rinse in cold water. Transfer to a large bowl and toss with the sesame oil.

Combine the sansho powder, oil and ¼ teaspoon salt and brush on both sides of the salmon. Heat a large frying pan over medium heat. Add the salmon and cook each side for 2–3 minutes, or until cooked to your liking. Remove from the pan and flake into large pieces with a fork.

Add the salmon, spring onion, coriander, cucumber and half the dressing to the noodles, then toss together. Place on a serving dish and drizzle with the remaining dressing.

Serves 4

Beef stroganoff

600 g rib eye fillet or rump
¼ cup (30 g) seasoned plain flour
375 g fettuccine or tagliatelle
60 g butter
1 small onion, finely chopped
300 g button mushrooms,
   thickly sliced
1 tablespoon tomato paste
   (tomato purée)
¼ cup (60 ml) red wine
300 ml cream

Pound the slices of beef between two sheets of plastic wrap with a mallet or rolling pin until half their thickness. Cut each slice into strips about 1 cm wide. Place in a plastic bag with the seasoned flour and shake to coat.

Cook the pasta in a large saucepan of rapidly boiling salted water until *al dente*.

Meanwhile, melt 40 g of the butter in a frying pan over medium heat and cook the onion for 2 minutes. Add the beef in batches and cook for 5 minutes, or until evenly browned. Remove from the pan and keep warm. Heat the remaining butter in the pan and add the mushrooms, stirring, for 2–3 minutes, or until soft and lightly browned. Add the tomato paste and the red wine, stirring continuously for 2 minutes, or until the sauce has reduced. Add the beef, stir in the cream, then reduce the heat to medium–low and simmer gently for another minute, or until the sauce has thickened. Serve with the pasta.

Serves 4

Mediterranean burgers

1 large red capsicum (pepper)
500 g lamb mince
1 egg, lightly beaten
1 small onion, grated
3 cloves garlic, crushed
2 tablespoons pine nuts, chopped
1 tablespoon finely chopped
  fresh mint
1 tablespoon finely chopped
  fresh flat-leaf parsley
1 teaspoon ground cumin
2 teaspoons chilli sauce
1 tablespoon olive oil
4 Turkish or pide bread rolls
1 cup (220 g) ready-made hummus
100 g baby rocket
1 small Lebanese cucumber,
  cut into ribbons
chilli sauce, to serve (optional)

Cut the capsicum into large pieces, removing the seeds and membrane. Place, skin-side-up, under a hot grill until the skin blackens and blisters. Cool in a plastic bag, then peel and cut into thick strips.

Combine the mince, egg, onion, garlic, pine nuts, fresh herbs, cumin and chilli sauce in a large bowl. Mix with your hands and roll into four even-sized balls. Press the balls into large patties about 9 cm in diameter.

Heat the oil in a large frying pan and cook the patties over medium heat for 6 minutes each side, or until well browned and cooked through, then drain on paper towels.

Halve the rolls and toast both sides. Spread the cut sides of the rolls with hummus, then lay rocket leaves, roasted capsicum and cucumber ribbons over the base. Place a patty on the salad and top with the other half of the roll. Serve with chilli sauce.

Serves 4

Chicken breasts with mustard cream sauce

4 chicken breasts (about 200 g each)
2 tablespoons oil
1 clove garlic, crushed
¼ cup (60 ml) dry white wine
2 tablespoons wholegrain mustard
2 teaspoons chopped fresh thyme
300 ml cream
240 g green beans, topped and tailed
320 g baby yellow squash, halved

Pound each chicken breast between sheets of plastic wrap with a mallet or rolling pin until about 1 cm thick.

Heat the oil in a frying pan over high heat. Brown the chicken breasts for 4–5 minutes on each side, or until brown. Remove and cover with foil.

Add the garlic to the frying pan and cook for 1 minute over medium heat, then stir in the wine, mustard and thyme. Increase the heat to medium–high and pour in the cream. Simmer for about 5 minutes, or until the sauce has reduced and thickened slightly, then season to taste.

Meanwhile, bring a saucepan of lightly salted water to the boil, add the beans and squash and cook for 2–4 minutes, or until just tender. Season to taste. To serve, pour a little of the sauce over the chicken and serve with the vegetables on the side.

Serves 4

Fish fillets with fennel and red capsicum salsa

750 g small new potatoes
1 teaspoon fennel seeds
½ cup (125 ml) olive oil
2 tablespoons drained baby capers
1 small red capsicum (pepper),
  seeded and finely diced
250 g mixed salad leaves, washed
  and picked over
2 tablespoons balsamic vinegar
4 white fish fillets (blue eye cod or
  John Dory), (about 200 g each)

Cook the potatoes in a saucepan of boiling water for 15–20 minutes, or until tender. Drain and keep warm.

Meanwhile, to make the salsa, dry-fry the fennel seeds in a frying pan over medium heat for 1 minute, or until fragrant. Remove the seeds and heat 1 tablespoon oil in the same pan over medium heat. When the oil is hot but not smoking, flash-fry the capers for 1–2 minutes, or until crisp. Remove from the pan. Heat 1 tablespoon oil and cook the capsicum, stirring, for 4–5 minutes, or until cooked through. Remove and combine with the fennel seeds and fried capers.

Place the salad leaves in a serving bowl. To make the dressing, combine the balsamic vinegar and ¼ cup (60 ml) of the olive oil in a bowl. Add 1 tablespoon to the salsa, then toss the rest through the salad leaves.

Wipe the frying pan, then heat the remaining oil over medium–high heat. Season the fish well. When the oil is hot, but not smoking, cook the fish for 2–3 minutes each side, or until cooked through. Serve immediately with the salsa, potatoes and salad.

Serves 4

Rare beef fillet with cellophane noodles and ginger dressing

400 g top-grade beef fillet
2 tablespoons peanut oil
250 g cellophane noodles
½ teaspoon sesame oil
2 spring onions, thinly sliced
  on the diagonal

Ginger dressing
1½ tablespoons finely chopped
  fresh ginger
3 tablespoons light soy sauce
3 tablespoons mirin
1 teaspoon sugar
2 teaspoons rice wine vinegar

Trim the beef of excess fat or sinew, then season with ground black pepper. Heat the peanut oil in a large frying pan. When very hot, sear the meat in batches on all sides for 3 minutes, or until brown. The meat needs to remain very pink on the inside. Remove from the frying pan and allow to cool. Cover and refrigerate until completely cold.

Place the noodles in a heatproof bowl, cover with boiling water and soak for 3–4 minutes. Drain and rinse under cold water. Return the noodles to the bowl, add the sesame oil and toss well together.

To make the ginger dressing, combine the chopped ginger in a small bowl with the light soy sauce, mirin, sugar and rice wine vinegar, stirring until the sugar has completely dissolved. Set aside until ready to use.

Add half the spring onion to the bowl of noodles, toss together well, then place on a large serving platter. Cut the beef into thin slices, then arrange in a mound on top of the noodles.

Warm the dressing slightly over low heat, then pour over the beef and noodles. Scatter with the remaining spring onion and serve immediately.

Serves 4

Pork chops with apple and red onion chutney

125 g butter
2 small red onions, sliced
2 Granny Smith apples, peeled, cored, then cut into quarters and sliced
¼ teaspoon ground cloves
⅓ cup (115 g) honey
4 pork loin chops (about 250 g each)
2 teaspoons oil
½ teaspoon caraway seeds
725 g green cabbage, thinly shredded

To make the chutney, melt 50 g of the butter in a saucepan, then add the onion, apple, cloves and honey. Simmer, covered, for 10 minutes over low heat. Increase the heat to medium, cover and cook for another 20 minutes, or until the liquid is reduced to a thick chutney. Allow to cool.

Meanwhile, season the chops well on both sides with salt and ground black pepper. Heat the oil and 50 g of the butter in a large frying pan and sauté the chops over medium–high heat for 6–8 minutes on each side, or until browned and cooked through. Remove the pan from the heat, leaving the chops to rest for 2 minutes.

While the chops are cooking, melt the remaining butter in a large saucepan, add the caraway seeds and cabbage and cook, covered, over medium–low heat, tossing a few times with tongs, for 12 minutes, or until tender.

To serve, place a pork chop on each plate and serve the cabbage on the side. Top with a spoonful of chutney.

Serves 4

Pan-fried lamb fillets with red wine

600 g small new potatoes
160 g snow peas (mangetout), trimmed
2 tablespoons olive oil
4 lamb backstraps or eye of loin fillets (about 200 g each), trimmed
2/3 cup (170 ml) red wine
1 tablespoon redcurrant jelly
2 teaspoons chopped fresh thyme
30 g butter, chilled and cut into cubes

Cook the potatoes in a large saucepan of lightly salted boiling water for 15–20 minutes, or until tender. Add the snow peas and cook for another minute. Drain the vegetables, return to the pan and toss gently with 1 tablespoon of the oil.

Meanwhile, heat the remaining oil in a large frying pan and cook the lamb fillets over medium–high heat for 4–5 minutes each side, or until cooked, but still pink inside. Remove from the pan, cover and keep warm.

Add the wine, redcurrant jelly and thyme to the pan and bring to the boil. Boil rapidly for 5 minutes, or until reduced and syrupy. Stir in the butter. To serve, slice the lamb on the diagonal, divide among four plates and spoon some sauce on top. Serve with the vegetables.

Serves 4

Sweet chilli and ginger swordfish

4 swordfish steaks
¼ cup (60 ml) peanut oil
3 cloves garlic, finely chopped
2 tablespoons grated fresh ginger
¼ cup (60 ml) lime juice
⅓ cup (80 ml) sweet chilli sauce

Place the swordfish steaks in a non-metallic bowl, brush lightly with a little of the oil and top each steak with some combined garlic and ginger.

Heat the remaining oil in a non-stick frying pan. Add the swordfish with the topping facing up. Cook over medium heat for 2 minutes, or until crisp and golden on the underside.

Combine 1 tablespoon each of the lime juice and sweet chilli sauce and drizzle over the steaks. Carefully turn over and cook for 2 minutes, or until tender but still pink in the middle. Remove and keep warm.

Add the remaining lime juice and sweet chilli sauce, bring to the boil and cook for 1 minute, or until the sauce is thickened. Serve with steamed rice and stir-fried vegetables.

Serves 4

Sausages and mash with French shallot gravy

⅓ cup (80 ml) olive oil
200 g French shallots, thinly sliced
1 tablespoon plain flour
½ cup (125 ml) red wine
1½ cups (375 ml) beef stock
1 tablespoon Dijon mustard
1.5 kg potatoes, chopped
150 g butter
8 thick pork sausages
  (about 100 g each)
450 g green beans, topped and tailed

Heat 2 tablespoons oil in a large frying pan over medium heat. Add the French shallots and cook for 5 minutes, stirring often until they soften. Add the flour and cook for 30 seconds. Increase the heat, pour in the wine and stock and bring to the boil. Reduce the heat and simmer for 10 minutes, or until the gravy thickens. Stir in the mustard, then reduce the heat to medium–low and simmer gently until the sausages and mash are ready.

Cook the potatoes in boiling water until tender. Drain, return to the pan and add 1 tablespoon olive oil and 120 g butter. Mash until smooth, then season with salt and black pepper.

While the potatoes are cooking, prick the sausages with a fork. Heat a large frying pan over medium–high heat, add the remaining oil and the sausages. Cook for 10 minutes, or until cooked through, turning often.

Bring a saucepan of lightly salted water to the boil, add the beans and cook for 4 minutes, or until just tender. Whisk the remaining butter into the gravy and season. Place a mound of mash on each plate, top with the sausages and gravy, and serve with the beans on the side.

Serves 4

Spanish saffron chicken and rice

¼ cup (60 ml) olive oil
4 chicken thighs and 6 drumsticks
1 large red onion, finely chopped
1 large green capsicum (pepper), two
    thirds diced and one third julienned
3 teaspoons sweet paprika
400 g can diced tomatoes
1¼ cups (275 g) paella or arborio rice
½ teaspoon ground saffron

Heat 2 tablespoons of the oil in a large deep frying pan over high heat. Season the chicken pieces well and brown in batches. Remove the chicken from the pan.

Reduce the pan to medium heat and add the remaining oil. Add the onion and the diced capsicum and cook gently for 5 minutes. Stir in the paprika and cook for 30 seconds. Add the tomato and simmer for 1–3 minutes, or until it thickens.

Stir 3½ cups (875 ml) boiling water into the pan, then add the rice and saffron. Return the chicken to the pan and stir to combine. Season, to taste. Bring to the boil, then cover, reduce the heat to medium–low and simmer for 20–30 minutes, or until all the liquid has been absorbed and the chicken is tender. Stir in the julienned capsicum, then allow to stand, covered, for 3–4 minutes before serving.

Serves 4

Classic omelette

12 eggs
40 g butter

Break the eggs into a bowl. Add 8 tablespoons water, season with salt and freshly ground black pepper, and beat together well. Heat 10 g of the butter in a small frying pan or omelette pan over high heat. When the butter is foaming, reduce the heat to medium and add one-quarter of the egg mixture. Tilt the pan to cover the base with the egg and leave for a few seconds. Using a spatula or egg flip, draw the sides of the omelette into the centre and let any extra liquid egg run to the edges.

If you are adding a filling to the omelette, sprinkle it over the egg. As soon as the egg is almost set, use an egg slide to fold the omelette in half in the pan. It should still be soft inside. Slide it onto a warm serving plate and repeat to make 3 more omelettes.

Serves 4

Fillings: Sprinkle each omelette with ⅓ cup (15 g) roughly torn rocket and 50 g crumbled goat's cheese.
   Saute 250 g finely sliced button mushrooms with 50 g butter, add 4 tablespoons finely chopped fresh basil and use some of the mixture for scattering over each omelette.

Veal scaloppine with sage

600 g small new potatoes, halved
⅓ cup (80 ml) olive oil
8 small (600 g) veal scaloppine fillets
  or schnitzels
4 slices pancetta, cut in half
8 fresh sage leaves
1 cup (250 ml) dry Marsala
250 g asparagus spears

Preheat the oven to moderately hot 200°C (400°F/Gas 6). Boil the potatoes for 10 minutes. Drain and transfer to a baking tray with 2 tablespoons olive oil. Toss well and bake for 40–50 minutes, or until crisp.

Pound each veal fillet between sheets of plastic wrap with a mallet until 5 mm thick. Press a piece of pancetta and a sage leaf onto each scaloppine fillet, then skewer with a toothpick. Season.

Heat the remaining oil in a large heavy-based frying pan. Place the scaloppine pancetta-side-down in the pan (do in batches if necessary) and cook for 1–2 minutes. Turn and cook for 1 minute. Remove from the pan and keep warm. Add the Marsala and cook for 4–5 minutes, or until syrupy and reduced by half. Return the scaloppine to the pan and toss lightly in the sauce until warmed through.

When the potatoes are nearly ready, bring a large saucepan of lightly salted water to the boil and cook the asparagus for 3 minutes. Drain.

Remove the toothpicks and divide the scaloppine among serving plates. Drizzle any pan juices on top. Serve with the asparagus and potatoes.

Serves 4

Tuna steaks with olive mayonnaise and potato wedges

3 large pontiac potatoes, unpeeled
and cut lengthways into 8 wedges
345 ml olive oil
2 egg yolks, at room temperature
25 ml lemon juice
1/3 cup (40 g) pitted black olives,
finely chopped
200 g baby rocket leaves
1 tablespoon finely chopped
fresh rosemary
4 tuna steaks (about 200 g each)

Preheat the oven to moderately hot 200°C (400°F/Gas 6). Toss the potatoes with 2 tablespoons oil in a baking tin. Bake for 45–50 minutes, or until crisp and golden.

Meanwhile, process the egg yolks in a food processor, adding 1/4 cup (60 ml) of the oil drop by drop. With the motor running, pour in 3/4 cup (185 ml) of the oil in a thin stream until the mixture thickens and becomes creamy. With the motor still running, add 1 teaspoon of the lemon juice, season with salt and blend for 30 seconds. Stir in the olives, cover and refrigerate.

To make the salad, toss the rocket leaves, 2 tablespoons oil and 1 tablespoon lemon juice in a bowl.

Press the rosemary into the tuna steaks. Heat the remaining tablespoon of oil in a large frying pan and sear the tuna steaks over medium–high heat for 2–3 minutes on each side, or until cooked to your liking. Serve with a dollop of olive mayonnaise, potato wedges and rocket salad.

Serves 4

Note: To save time, use 1 cup (250 g) of good-quality whole-egg mayonnaise.

Parmesan chicken with quick salsa verde

3 eggs
1 cup (30 g) loosely packed
 fresh basil
2 tablespoons capers, rinsed
1 tablespoon Dijon mustard
2 tablespoons freshly grated
 Parmesan
3/4 cup (185 ml) olive oil
1 cup (100 g) dry breadcrumbs
4 chicken breast fillets
 (about 120 g each)
150 g rocket leaves
lemon wedges, to serve

Place 1 egg in a saucepan of cold water, bring to the boil and cook for 1 minute. Remove from the heat and refresh under cold water. Peel, then place in a food processor with the basil, capers, mustard and 1 tablespoon of the Parmesan, until combined. Gradually add 1/4 cup (60 ml) of the olive oil and process until you have a coarse sauce, taking care not to overprocess.

Beat the remaining eggs together with 1 tablespoon water. Combine the breadcrumbs with the remaining Parmesan on a plate. Pound each chicken breast between two sheets of plastic wrap with a mallet or rolling pin until 5 mm thick. Dip the chicken in the egg mixture, then coat in the breadcrumb mixture. Place on a paper-lined baking tray and refrigerate for 10 minutes, or until needed.

Heat the remaining oil in a large frying pan over high heat. Cook the chicken breasts in batches for 2–3 minutes each batch, or until golden on both sides and cooked through—keep each batch warm. Serve with the salsa verde, rocket leaves and lemon wedges.

Serves 4

Fillet steaks with pink peppercorn sauce

60 g butter
1 tablespoon oil
4 fillet steaks, rump or New York
  cut, trimmed
½ cup (125 ml) white wine
2 tablespoons brandy
½ cup (125 ml) beef stock
2 tablespoons pink peppercorns
  in brine, drained and rinsed
½ cup (125 ml) cream

Heat the butter and oil in a large frying pan, and cook the steaks over high heat for 3–4 minutes each side, or until cooked to your liking. Remove from the pan, cover and keep warm.

Add the wine and brandy to the pan, and simmer for 4 minutes, or until reduced by half. Add the beef stock and reduce by half again (you should have just over ½ cup/125 ml sauce). Meanwhile, roughly chop half the peppercorns.

Stir in all the peppercorns and the cream, and cook gently until the sauce has thickened slightly. Place the steaks on four warmed serving plates and spoon the sauce over the top. Serve with a green salad.

Serves 4

Veal schnitzel with dill potato salad

750 g desiree potatoes, unpeeled
500 g veal leg steaks
½ cup (60 g) seasoned plain flour
2 eggs, lightly beaten
1 cup (100 g) dry breadcrumbs
½ cup (125 ml) virgin olive oil
2 tablespoons lemon juice
1½ tablespoons finely chopped
   fresh dill
200 g mixed salad leaves

Cook the potatoes in a large saucepan of boiling water for 15–20 minutes, or until tender. Drain, then cut into quarters lengthways and cover to keep warm.

Meanwhile, beat the veal between two sheets of plastic wrap to 5 mm thickness. Coat the veal in the flour and shake off the excess. Dip the veal in the egg, then coat in breadcrumbs. Place the schnitzel on a flat tray, cover and freeze for 5 minutes.

Heat ¼ cup (60 ml) of the oil in a large frying pan and cook the veal in two batches, over medium–high heat for 2–3 minutes on each side, or until golden and cooked through. Drain on crumpled paper towels and keep warm.

Whisk the lemon juice, dill and remaining oil together in a small bowl and pour over the potatoes. Season with salt and freshly ground black pepper and toss gently. Serve the schnitzel with the potatoes and a mixed salad.

Serves 4

Seared salmon with sesame and cucumber noodles

250 g buckwheat soba noodles
1½ tablespoons sesame oil
2 tablespoons kecap manis
1 tablespoon Chinese black vinegar
2 Lebanese cucumbers, julienned
6 spring onions, trimmed and sliced
    on the diagonal into 4 cm lengths
2 tablespoons black sesame seeds
600 g salmon fillet pieces, skinned
    and boned

Cook the noodles in a large saucepan of boiling water until tender—this should take about 5 minutes. Drain well. Place in a large bowl and mix in 2 teaspoons of the sesame oil, then set aside to cool. Combine the kecap manis, vinegar and the remaining sesame oil, then toss 1 tablespoon of the mixture through the noodles. Cover the noodles and refrigerate for about 2 hours.

About 20 minutes before serving, gently mix the noodles with the cucumber, spring onion and black sesame seeds.

Heat a large frying pan over medium–high heat. Brush the salmon pieces lightly with oil and season with salt and freshly ground black pepper. Cook for 1–2 minutes on each side, or until cooked to your liking. Remove from the heat and allow to cool until cool enough to handle. Flake the fish into large pieces and gently incorporate it into the noodles, along with the rest of the dressing—be careful not to over-handle or the salmon will flake into small pieces. Serve immediately.

Serves 4

Note: These noodles need marinating for 2 hours but the rest of the preparation is very quick.

Eggplant, tomato and goat's cheese stacks

½ cup (125 ml) olive oil
2 large cloves garlic, crushed
2 small eggplants (aubergine)
2 ripe tomatoes
150 g goat's cheese
8 basil leaves
small rocket leaves, to garnish

Dressing
285 g jar sun-dried tomatoes,
    drained, reserving 1 tablespoon oil
1 clove garlic, crushed
2 tablespoons white wine vinegar
2 tablespoons whole-egg mayonnaise

Place the oil and garlic in a bowl and mix together. Cut each eggplant into six 1 cm slices, then cut each tomato into four 1 cm slices. Using a sharp knife dipped in hot water, cut the cheese into eight 1 cm slices.

Brush both sides of the eggplant with half of the oil mixture. Heat a frying pan and cook the eggplant in batches over high heat for 3–4 minutes each side, or until golden. Remove and keep warm. Brush both sides of the tomato with the remaining oil mixture and cook for 1 minute each side, or until sealed and warmed through.

To make the dressing, blend the sun-dried tomatoes, reserved oil and the garlic in a food processor until smooth. Add the vinegar and process until combined. Transfer to a bowl and stir in the mayonnaise. Season.

To assemble, place an eggplant slice on each plate. Top with a slice of tomato, then a basil leaf and a slice of cheese. Repeat with the remaining ingredients to give two layers, then finish with a third piece of eggplant. Add a dollop of dressing and arrange the rocket around each stack. Serve immediately.

Serves 4

Lemon pepper tuna burger

2 x 185 g cans lemon pepper tuna, drained
1 large onion, chopped
2/3 cup (65 g) dry breadcrumbs
1 egg, lightly beaten
2 tablespoons chopped fresh lemon thyme
1 tablespoon chopped fresh flat-leaf parsley
2 teaspoons grated lemon rind
2 tablespoons oil
1 loaf Turkish bread
1/3 cup (80 g) whole-egg mayonnaise
150 g rocket
4 slices Cheddar cheese
2 tomatoes, sliced
1 cucumber, sliced
1/2 red onion, sliced

Mix the tuna, onion, breadcrumbs, egg, thyme, parsley and lemon rind in a bowl. Form into four even-sized patties and flatten slightly. Heat a non-stick frying pan with the oil. Cook the patties over medium heat on both sides for 5 minutes, or until browned.

Cut the bread into 4 portions. Cut each portion in half horizontally and place under a grill to lightly brown.

Spread both cut sides of the bread with mayonnaise. Top with some rocket and layer with a patty, a slice of cheese and slices of tomato, cucumber and onion. Place the other half of the Turkish bread on top, cut in half and serve.

Serves 4

Crab, Camembert and fusilli frittata

1 cup (80 g) tri-coloured fusilli
1 tablespoon olive oil
1 very small red onion, finely chopped
1 large Roma tomato, roughly chopped
1/3 cup (60 g) semi-dried tomatoes, roughly chopped
2 tablespoons finely chopped fresh coriander leaves
2/3 cup (140 g) cooked fresh or canned crab meat
150 g Camembert, rind removed, cut into small pieces
6 eggs plus 2 egg yolks

Cook the pasta in a large saucepan of rapidly boiling salted water until *al dente*. Drain, rinse, then drain again and set aside to cool. Meanwhile, heat half the oil in a small frying pan over low heat, add the onion and cook for 4–5 minutes, or until softened but not browned. Transfer to a bowl and add the Roma tomato, semi-dried tomatoes and coriander. Squeeze out any excess moisture from the crab meat and add the meat to the bowl. Add half the cheese to the bowl, then add the cooled pasta. Mix well. Beat together the six eggs and the two extra yolks, then stir into the tomato and crab mixture. Season.

Heat the remaining oil in the frying pan, pour in the frittata mixture and cook over low heat for 25 minutes. Preheat the grill to low. Scatter the remaining Camembert over the frittata before placing it under the grill for 10–15 minutes, or until cooked and golden brown on top. Remove from the grill and leave for 5 minutes. Cut into slices and serve with salad and some bread.

Serves 4–6

Note: Although this recipe can be prepared very quickly, it does take a while to cook.

Orange sweet potato and ditalini patties

2 orange sweet potatoes
  (about 800 g in total)
½ cup (90 g) ditalini
30 g toasted pine nuts
2 cloves garlic, crushed
4 tablespoons finely chopped
  fresh basil
½ cup (50 g) grated Parmesan
⅓ cup (35 g) dry breadcrumbs
plain flour, for dusting
olive oil, for shallow-frying

Preheat the oven to very hot 250°C (500°F/Gas 10). Pierce the whole orange sweet potatoes several times with a fork, then place in a roasting tin and roast for 1 hour, or until soft. Remove and allow to cool. Meanwhile, cook the pasta in a large saucepan of rapidly boiling salted water until *al dente*. Drain and rinse under running water.

Peel the sweet potato and mash the flesh with a potato masher or fork, then add the pine nuts, garlic, basil, Parmesan, breadcrumbs and the pasta and combine. Season.

Shape the mixture into eight even patties (about 1.5 cm thick) with floured hands, then lightly dust the patties with flour. Heat the oil in a large frying pan and cook the patties in batches over medium heat for 2 minutes each side, or until golden and heated through. Drain on crumpled paper towels, sprinkle with salt and serve immediately. Great with a fresh green salad.

Serves 4

Note: Roasting the sweet potato is the most time-consuming part of this recipe and you don't need to be in the kitchen the whole time they are cooking. The rest is easy.

Wok

Beef and bamboo shoots

¼ cup (60 ml) oil
400 g rump steak,
  thinly sliced across the grain
227 g can sliced bamboo shoots,
  drained and rinsed
3 cloves garlic, crushed with
  ¼ teaspoon salt
2 tablespoons fish sauce
8 spring onions, cut into 4 cm
  lengths on the diagonal
¼ cup (40 g) sesame seeds, toasted

Heat a wok over high heat, add 2 tablespoons of the oil and swirl. When the oil is hot, add the beef in two batches and stir-fry for 1 minute, or until it starts to turn pink. Remove and set aside.

Add an extra tablespoon of oil if necessary, then stir-fry the bamboo shoots for 3 minutes, or until starting to brown. Add the garlic, fish sauce and ¼ teaspoon salt and stir-fry for 2–3 minutes. Add the spring onion and stir-fry for 1 minute, or until starting to wilt. Return the beef to the wok, stir quickly and cook for 1 minute until heated through. Remove from the heat, toss with the sesame seeds and serve with rice.

Serves 4

Orange sweet potato, spinach and water chestnut stir-fry

500 g orange sweet potato
1 tablespoon oil
2 cloves garlic, crushed
2 teaspoons sambal oelek
227 g can water chestnuts, sliced
2 teaspoons grated palm sugar
390 g English spinach, stems
  removed
2 tablespoons soy sauce
2 tablespoons vegetable stock

Cut the orange sweet potato into 1.5 cm x 1.5 cm cubes. Cook the sweet potato in a large saucepan of boiling water for 15 minutes, or until tender. Drain well.

Heat a wok until very hot, add the oil and swirl to coat. Stir-fry the garlic and sambal oelek for 1 minute, or until fragrant. Add the sweet potato and water chestnuts and stir-fry over medium–high heat for 2 minutes. Reduce the heat to medium, add the palm sugar and cook for another 2 minutes, or until the sugar has melted. Add the spinach, soy sauce and stock and toss until the spinach has just wilted. Serve with rice.

Serves 4

Note: Sambal oelek is made from mashed fresh red chillies mixed with salt and vinegar or tamarind. Palm sugar is available from most large supermarkets in jars or wrapped in paper. Use demerara or soft brown sugar if not available.

Prawns with spicy tamarind sauce

½ cup (80 g) raw cashew nuts
1¼ cups (250 g) jasmine rice
2 garlic cloves, finely chopped
1½ tablespoons fish sauce
1 tablespoon sambal oelek
1 tablespoon peanut oil
1 kg raw medium prawns, peeled
  and deveined with tails intact
2 teaspoons tamarind concentrate
1½ tablespoons grated palm sugar
350 g choy sum, cut into
  10 cm lengths

Preheat the oven to moderate 180°C (350°F/Gas 4). Spread the cashews on a baking tray and bake for 5–8 minutes, or until light golden — watch carefully, as they burn easily.

Meanwhile, bring a large saucepan of water to the boil. Add the rice and cook for 12 minutes, stirring occasionally. Drain well.

Place the garlic, fish sauce, sambal oelek and toasted cashews in a blender or food processor, adding 2–3 tablespoons of water, if needed, and blend to a rough paste.

Heat a wok until very hot, add the oil and swirl to coat. Add the prawns, toss for 1–2 minutes, or until starting to turn pink. Remove from the wok. Add the cashew paste and stir-fry for 1 minute, or until it starts to brown slightly. Add the tamarind, sugar and about ⅓ cup (80 ml) water, then bring to the boil, stirring well. Return the prawns to the wok and stir to coat. Cook for 2–3 minutes, or until the prawns are cooked through.

Place the choy sum in a paper-lined bamboo steamer and steam over a wok or saucepan of simmering water for 3 minutes, or until tender. Serve with the prawns and rice.

Serves 4

Stir-fried hoisin pork and greens with gingered rice

1¼ cups (250 g) jasmine rice
500 g pork fillets, thinly sliced
1 tablespoon caster sugar
2 tablespoons oil
½ cup (125 ml) white wine vinegar
1 cup (250 ml) hoisin sauce
2 tablespoons stem ginger in syrup, chopped
1.25 kg mixed Asian greens (bok choy, choy sum or spinach)

Rinse the rice and place in a large saucepan. Add 1¾ cups (435 ml) water and bring to the boil. Cover, reduce the heat to very low and cook for 10 minutes. Remove from the heat and leave to stand, covered, for 10 minutes.

Meanwhile, place the pork in a bowl and sprinkle with the sugar. Toss to coat. Heat a wok over high heat, add 1 tablespoon oil and swirl to coat. Add the pork in batches and stir-fry for 3 minutes, or until brown. Remove. Add the vinegar to the wok and boil for 3–5 minutes, or until reduced by two-thirds. Reduce the heat, add the hoisin sauce and 1 tablespoon ginger, and simmer for 5 minutes. Season to taste. Remove from the wok.

Reheat the cleaned wok over high heat, add the remaining oil and swirl to coat. Add the greens and stir-fry for 3 minutes, or until crisp and cooked. Stir the remaining ginger through the rice, then press into four round teacups or small Asian bowls, smoothing the surface. Unmould the rice onto four serving plates, arrange the pork and greens on the side and drizzle the sauce over the top.

Serves 4

Beef and hokkien noodle stir-fry

350 g beef fillet, partially frozen
100 g snow peas (mangetout)
600 g fresh Hokkien noodles
1 tablespoon peanut oil
1 large onion, cut into thin wedges
1 large carrot, thinly sliced
  on the diagonal
1 medium red capsicum (pepper),
  cut into thin strips
2 cloves garlic, crushed
1 teaspoon grated fresh ginger
200 g fresh shiitake mushrooms,
  sliced
1/4 cup (60 ml) oyster sauce
2 tablespoons light soy sauce
1 tablespoon soft brown sugar
1/2 teaspoon five-spice powder

Cut the steak into thin slices. Top and tail the snow peas and slice in half diagonally. Soak the noodles in a large bowl with enough boiling water to cover for 10 minutes.

Spray a large wok with oil spray and when very hot, cook the steak in batches until brown. Remove and keep warm.

Heat the peanut oil in the wok, and when very hot, stir-fry the onion, carrot and capsicum for 2–3 minutes, or until tender. Add the garlic, ginger, snow peas and shiitake mushrooms, and cook for another minute before returning the steak to the wok.

Separate the noodles with a fork, then drain. Add to the wok, tossing well. Combine the oyster sauce with the soy sauce, brown sugar, five-spice powder and 1 tablespoon water and pour over the noodles. Toss until warmed through, then serve.

Serves 4

Calamari in black bean and chilli sauce

4 squid tubes
2 tablespoons oil
1 onion, cut into 8 wedges
1 red capsicum (pepper), sliced
115 g baby corn, cut in halves
3 spring onions, optional, cut into
  3 cm lengths

Black bean sauce
3 teaspoons cornflour
2 tablespoons canned salted black
  beans, washed, drained
2 small red chillies, seeded
  and chopped
2 cloves garlic, finely chopped
2 teaspoons grated fresh ginger
2 tablespoons oyster sauce
2 teaspoons soy sauce
1 teaspoon sugar

Open out each squid hood. Score a shallow diamond pattern over the inside surface of each, without cutting through, then cut into 5 cm squares.

For the sauce, mix the cornflour with ½ cup (125 ml) water in a small bowl. Place the black beans in a bowl and mash with a fork. Add the chilli, garlic, ginger, oyster and soy sauces, sugar and the cornflour mix and stir.

Heat the oil in a wok and stir the onion for 1 minute over high heat. Add the capsicum and corn and stir for another 2 minutes.

Add the squid to the wok and stir for 1–2 minutes, until the flesh curls up. Add the sauce and bring to the boil, stirring constantly until the sauce thickens. Stir in the spring onion. Serve with steamed rice noodles.

Serves 4

Note: Instead of squid, you can use fish, cuttlefish, prawns, octopus, or a combination.

Chicken with Thai basil

3 tablespoons peanut oil
500 g chicken breast fillets, trimmed
    and cut into thin strips
1 clove garlic, crushed
4 spring onions, thinly sliced
150 g snake beans, trimmed
    and cut into 5 cm lengths
2 small fresh red chillies, thinly sliced
3/4 cup (35 g) tightly packed fresh
    Thai basil
2 tablespoons chopped fresh mint
1 tablespoon fish sauce
1 tablespoon oyster sauce
2 teaspoons lime juice
1 tablespoon grated palm sugar
fresh Thai basil, extra, to garnish

Heat a wok over high heat, add
1 tablespoon of the oil and swirl to
coat. Cook the chicken in batches for
3–5 minutes, or until lightly browned
and almost cooked — add more oil if
needed. Remove and keep warm.

Heat the remaining oil. Add the garlic,
onion, snake beans and chilli, and
stir-fry for 1 minute, or until the onion
is tender. Add the chicken to the wok.

Toss in the basil and mint, then add
the combined fish sauce, oyster
sauce, lime juice, palm sugar and
2 tablespoons water and cook for
1 minute. Garnish with the extra basil
and serve with jasmine rice.

Serves 4

Red roast duck curry

1 tablespoon peanut oil
2 cloves garlic, crushed
8 spring onions, cut into 3 cm lengths
1 tablespoon red curry paste, or to
    taste
400 ml coconut milk
750 g Chinese roast duck, chopped
450 g can pineapple pieces in syrup,
    drained
3 fresh kaffir lime leaves
¼ cup (15 g) chopped fresh coriander
    leaves
2 tablespoons chopped fresh mint

Heat a wok until very hot, add the oil
and swirl to coat. Add the garlic,
spring onion and paste and stir-fry
for 1 minute, or until fragrant.

Stir in the coconut milk, duck,
pineapple, lime leaves, coriander
leaves and mint. Bring to the boil,
then reduce the heat and simmer
for 10 minutes, or until the duck
is heated through. Serve with
jasmine rice.

Serves 4–6

Lamb, mint and chilli stir-fry

1¼ cups (250 g) jasmine rice
2 tablespoons oil
750 g lamb backstrap or eye of loin
  fillets, sliced thinly
2 cloves garlic, finely chopped
1 small red onion, cut into wedges
1 fresh bird's eye chilli, finely chopped
¼ cup (60 ml) lime juice
2 tablespoons sweet chilli sauce
2 tablespoons fish sauce
½ cup (10 g) fresh mint leaves

Bring a large saucepan of water to the boil. Add the rice and cook for 12 minutes, stirring occasionally. Drain well.

Meanwhile, heat a wok until very hot, add 1 tablespoon oil and swirl to coat. Add the lamb in batches and cook for 2 minutes, or until browned. Remove from the wok.

Heat the remaining oil in the wok, add the garlic and onion and stir-fry for 1 minute, then add the chilli and cook for 30 seconds. Return the lamb to the wok, then add the lime juice, sweet chilli sauce and fish sauce and stir-fry for 2 minutes over high heat. Stir in the mint and serve with the rice.

Serves 4

Note: You can use chicken breasts or pork loin, adding ½ cup (80 g) cashews and using basil instead of mint.

Fried rice with Chinese barbecue pork

6 spring onions
150 g snow peas (mangetout)
200 g Chinese barbecue pork
3 teaspoons sesame oil
2 eggs, lightly beaten
2 cloves garlic, finely chopped
3 cups (555 g) cold cooked white
   long-grain rice (see Note)
2 tablespoons soy sauce

Cut the spring onions and snow peas diagonally into very thin shreds. Cut the pork into thin slices.

Heat a wok until hot, add 1 teaspoon of the oil and swirl to coat the base. Add the egg and swirl over the base until just set. Turn over and cook for 30 seconds, or until just lightly browned, then remove from the wok. Allow the egg to cool slightly, then roll up and cut into 1 cm thick slices.

While the wok is still very hot, add the remaining oil, then the garlic, spring onion and snow peas and stir-fry for 1–2 minutes, or until slightly soft. Add the pork, rice, soy sauce and strips of omelette and toss until heated through and thoroughly combined — the soy sauce should turn the rice brown. Remove from the heat and serve immediately.

Serves 4

Note: Cook 1 cup (200 g) long-grain rice in a large saucepan of boiling water. To cool, spread the rice on a shallow tray and leave uncovered overnight in the refrigerator.

Chilli snake beans and noodles

325 g fresh flat egg noodles
  (5 mm wide)
5 cloves garlic, peeled
3 red Asian shallots, chopped
1 small fresh red chilli, seeded
  and chopped
3 fresh coriander roots, chopped
2½ tablespoons peanut oil
500 g snake beans, cut into
  4 cm lengths
2½ tablespoons fish sauce
1½ tablespoons grated palm
  sugar
1 tablespoon kecap manis
1 tablespoon lime juice
1 tablespoon crisp fried
  onion flakes

Cook the noodles in a saucepan of boiling water for 1 minute, or until tender. Drain well.

Place the garlic, red Asian shallots, chilli and coriander roots in a mortar and pestle or small food processor and grind to a smooth paste—add a little water if necessary.

Heat a wok over high heat, add the oil and swirl to coat. Stir in the paste and cook for 1 minute, or until fragrant. Add the beans, stir-fry for 2 minutes, then reduce the heat to low, cover and steam for 2 minutes. Increase the heat to high, add the fish sauce, palm sugar and kecap manis and stir-fry for 1 minute. Toss the noodles through the bean mixture for 1–2 minutes, or until heated through. Drizzle with the lime juice. Divide among serving bowls. If you wish, serve with lime wedges and garnish with the crisp fried onion flakes and sliced chilli.

Serves 4

Water spinach in flames

4 cloves garlic, crushed
2 medium fresh green chillies,
　finely sliced
1 tablespoon black bean sauce
2 tablespoons fish sauce
2 teaspoons sugar
2 tablespoons oil
500 g water spinach, cut into
　3 cm lengths

Place the garlic, chilli, black bean
sauce, fish sauce and sugar in a bowl
and mix together well.

Heat a wok over high heat, add the oil
and swirl to coat. Add the spinach
and stir-fry for 1 minute, or until wilted
slightly. Add the sauce and stir-fry for
30 seconds, or until the spinach
leaves are coated. Serve immediately.

Serves 4

Note: English spinach can be used
instead of the water spinach.

Spring onion lamb

600 g lean lamb backstraps or eye of
loin fillets, sliced across the grain
into very thin slices
1 tablespoon Chinese rice wine
or dry sherry
¼ cup (60 ml) soy sauce
½ teaspoon white pepper
6 spring onions
1½ cups (300 g) long-grain rice
2 tablespoons oil
750 g choy sum, cut into
10 cm lengths
3 cloves garlic, crushed
1 tablespoon Chinese black vinegar
1 teaspoon sesame oil

Put the lamb in a non-metallic bowl
with the rice wine, 1 tablespoon soy
sauce, ½ teaspoon salt and the white
pepper and mix. Cover and chill for
10 minutes. Slice the spring onions
diagonally into 4 cm lengths.

Meanwhile, bring a large pan of water
to the boil. Add the rice and cook for
12 minutes, stirring occasionally. Drain.

Heat a wok over high heat, add
½ tablespoon oil and swirl to coat.
Add the choy sum, stir-fry, then add
1 clove garlic and 1 tablespoon soy
sauce. Cook for 3 minutes, or until
crisp. Take the wok off the heat,
remove the greens and keep warm.

Wipe out the wok and heat over high
heat, then add 1 tablespoon oil and
swirl. Add the lamb in batches and
stir-fry over high heat for 1–2 minutes,
or until brown. Remove from the wok.

Add more oil to the wok if necessary.
Add the spring onion and remaining
garlic and stir-fry for 1–2 minutes.
Combine the vinegar, sesame oil and
the remaining soy sauce. Pour into
the wok, stirring for 1 minute. Return
the lamb to the wok and stir-fry for
another minute, or until combined and
heated through. Serve immediately
with the stir-fried greens and rice.

Serves 4

Eggplant and buckwheat noodle salad

10 g dried shiitake mushrooms
350 g buckwheat (soba) noodles
2 teaspoons sesame oil
3 tablespoons tahini
1 tablespoon light soy sauce
1 tablespoon dark soy sauce
1 tablespoon honey
2 tablespoons lemon juice
3 tablespoons peanut oil
2 Japanese eggplants (aubergine),
  cut into very thin strips
2 carrots, julienned
10 spring onions, cut on
  the diagonal
6 fresh shiitake mushrooms,
  thinly sliced
1 cup (50 g) roughly chopped
  fresh coriander leaves

Soak the dried shiitake mushrooms in ½ cup (125 ml) hot water for 10 minutes. Drain, reserving the liquid. Discard the woody stems and finely slice the caps.

Cook the noodles in a saucepan of boiling water for 5 minutes, or until tender. Drain. Refresh under cold water then toss with 1 teaspoon of the sesame oil.

Combine the tahini, light and dark soy sauces, honey, lemon juice, 2 tablespoons of the reserved mushroom liquid and the remaining sesame oil in a food processor until smooth.

Heat 2 tablespoons of the peanut oil in a wok over high heat. Add the eggplant and cook, turning often, for 4–5 minutes, or until soft and golden. Drain on paper towels.

Heat the remaining oil. Add the carrot, spring onion and fresh and dried mushrooms. Cook, stirring constantly, for 1–2 minutes, or until just softened. Remove from the heat and toss with the noodles, eggplant and dressing. Garnish with the coriander.

Serves 4–6

Tiger prawn and rice noodle salad

Dressing
2 tablespoons dark soy sauce
1 tablespoon fish sauce
2 tablespoons lime juice
1 teaspoon grated lime rind
1 teaspoon caster sugar
1 fresh red chilli, seeded and
    finely chopped
2 teaspoons finely chopped
    fresh ginger

150 g dried rice vermicelli
100 g snow peas (mangetout),
    trimmed, cut in half widthways
3 tablespoons peanut oil
2/3 cup (100 g) raw cashews,
    chopped
24 raw tiger prawns, peeled,
    deveined and tails intact
1/2 cup (10 g) fresh mint, chopped
1/2 cup (15 g) fresh coriander leaves,
    chopped

To make the dressing, combine the ingredients in a small bowl.

Soak the noodles in boiling water for 6–7 minutes. Drain and set aside.

Blanch the snow peas in boiling salted water for 10 seconds. Drain and refresh in cold water.

Heat the oil in a wok and swirl to coat. When hot, add the cashews and stir-fry for 2–3 minutes, or until golden. Remove with a slotted spoon and drain on paper towels. Add the prawns to the wok and cook over high heat, stirring constantly, for 2–3 minutes, or until just pink. Transfer to a large bowl, pour on the dressing and toss. Chill.

Add the noodles, snow peas, mint, coriander and cashews, toss well and serve immediately.

Serves 4

Stir-fried mixed vegetables

2 tablespoons oil
4 spring onions, cut into 3 cm lengths
3 cloves garlic, crushed
1 fresh red chilli, seeded and sliced
75 g button mushrooms, quartered
100 g Chinese cabbage,
  roughly chopped
2 tablespoons soy sauce
1 teaspoon fish sauce
1 tablespoon oyster sauce
¼ cup (60 ml) vegetable stock
½ teaspoon grated palm sugar
150 g snow peas (mangetout)
150 g cauliflower, cut into small florets
150 g broccoli, cut into small florets
fresh coriander leaves, chopped,
  to garnish

Heat a wok until very hot, add the oil and swirl to coat. Add the spring onion, garlic and chilli. Stir-fry for 20 seconds. Add the mushrooms and cabbage and stir-fry for 1 minute.

Stir in the sauces, stock, palm sugar, snow peas, cauliflower and broccoli. Cook for 2 minutes, or until tender. Garnish with the coriander leaves.

Serves 6

Lemon grass beef

1½ cups (300 g) long-grain rice
3 cloves garlic, finely chopped
1 tablespoon grated fresh ginger
4 stems lemon grass (white part only),
  finely chopped
2½ tablespoons oil
600 g lean rump steak, trimmed and
  sliced thinly across the grain
1 tablespoon lime juice
1–2 tablespoons fish sauce
2 tablespoons kecap manis
1 large red onion, cut into
  small wedges
200 g green beans, sliced on the
  diagonal into 5 cm lengths

Bring a large saucepan of water to
the boil. Add the rice and cook for
12 minutes, stirring occasionally.
Drain well.

Meanwhile, combine the garlic,
ginger, lemon grass and 2 teaspoons
of the oil in a non-metallic bowl.
Add the beef, then marinate for
10 minutes. Combine the lime juice,
fish sauce and kecap manis.

Heat a wok until very hot, add
1 tablespoon oil and swirl to coat.
Stir-fry the beef in batches for
2–3 minutes, or until browned.
Remove from the wok.

Reheat the wok to very hot, heat the
remaining oil, then add the onion and
stir-fry for 2 minutes. Add the beans
and cook for another 2 minutes, then
return the beef to the wok. Pour in the
fish sauce mixture and cook until
heated through. Serve with the rice.

Serves 4

Caramel pork and pumpkin stir-fry

1¼ cups (250 g) jasmine rice
500 g pork fillet, thinly sliced
2 cloves garlic, crushed
2–3 tablespoons peanut oil
300 g butternut pumpkin,
    cut into 2 cm x 4 cm pieces
    about 5 mm thick
⅓ cup (60 g) soft brown sugar
¼ cup (60 ml) fish sauce
¼ cup (60 ml) rice vinegar
2 tablespoons chopped fresh
    coriander leaves
1.25 kg mixed Asian greens
    (bok choy, choy sum, gai larn)

Bring a large saucepan of water to the boil. Add the rice and cook for 12 minutes, stirring occasionally. Drain.

Combine the pork with the garlic and 2 teaspoons of the peanut oil. Season with salt and plenty of pepper.

Heat a wok until very hot, add 1 tablespoon oil and swirl to coat. When just starting to smoke, stir-fry the pork in two batches for about 1 minute per batch, or until the meat changes colour. Transfer to a plate. Add the remaining oil to the wok and stir-fry the pumpkin for 4 minutes, or until tender but not falling apart. Remove and add to the pork.

Combine the sugar, fish sauce, rice vinegar and ½ cup (125 ml) water in the wok and boil for about 10 minutes, or until syrupy. Return the pork and pumpkin to the wok and stir for 1 minute, or until well coated and heated through. Stir in the coriander.

Put the mixed Asian greens in a paper-lined bamboo steamer over a wok of simmering water for 3 minutes, or until wilted. Serve immediately with the stir-fry and rice.

Serves 4

Tofu, snow pea and mushroom stir-fry

1 1/4 cups (250 g) jasmine rice
1/4 cup (60 ml) peanut oil
600 g firm tofu, drained, cut
  into 2 cm cubes
2 teaspoons sambal oelek
  or chilli paste
2 cloves garlic, finely chopped
400 g fresh Asian mushrooms, sliced
  (shiitake, oyster or black fungus)
300 g snow peas (mangetout),
  trimmed
1/4 cup (60 ml) kecap manis

Bring a large saucepan of water to the boil. Add the rice and cook for 12 minutes, stirring occasionally. Drain well.

Meanwhile, heat a wok until very hot. Add 2 tablespoons of the oil and swirl to coat. Stir-fry the tofu in two batches on all sides for 2–3 minutes, or until lightly browned, then transfer to a plate.

Add the remaining oil to the wok, add the sambal oelek, garlic, mushrooms, snow peas and 1 tablespoon water and stir-fry for 1–2 minutes, or until the vegetables are almost cooked but still crunchy.

Return the tofu to the wok, add the kecap manis and stir-fry for a minute, or until heated through and combined. Serve immediately with the rice.

Serves 4

Ginger chicken stir-fry with hokkien noodles

2½ tablespoons finely shredded fresh ginger
¼ cup (60 ml) mirin
2 tablespoons soy sauce
600 g chicken tenderloins or chicken breast fillets, cut diagonally into thin strips
180 g fresh baby corn
350 g choy sum
150 g fresh oyster mushrooms
500 g Hokkien noodles, gently separated
2 tablespoons oil
2 tablespoons oyster sauce

Combine the ginger, mirin and soy sauce in a non-metallic bowl. Add the chicken, coat well, then marinate while preparing the vegetables.

Cut the corn in half lengthways; trim the ends off the choy sum and cut into 6 cm lengths. If the mushrooms are very large, cut them in half. Soak the noodles in a large heatproof bowl in boiling water for 5 minutes. Drain and refresh under cold running water.

Heat a wok until very hot, add 1 tablespoon of the oil and swirl to coat. Remove the chicken from the marinade with a slotted spoon and cook in two batches over very high heat for 2 minutes, or until brown and just cooked. Remove from the wok.

Add the remaining oil to the wok and stir-fry the mushrooms and corn for 1–2 minutes, or until just softened. Add the remaining marinade, bring to the boil, then add the chicken, choy sum and noodles. Stir in the oyster sauce and cook, tossing well, for 1–2 minutes, or until the choy sum has wilted slightly and the noodles are warmed through.

Serves 4

Prawn rice noodle rolls

1 tablespoon peanut oil
2 cloves garlic, crushed
200 g fresh shiitake mushrooms,
  thinly sliced
5 spring onions, chopped
1/3 cup (60 g) drained and chopped
  water chestnuts
150 g fresh baby corn, roughly
  chopped
650 g raw medium prawns, peeled,
  deveined and roughly chopped
500 g fresh rice noodle rolls
oil, for brushing

Sauce
1/4 cup (60 ml) light soy sauce
2 teaspoons sesame oil
1 teaspoon grated fresh ginger
1 teaspoon sugar
2 tablespoons Chinese rice wine

Heat a wok over high heat, add the oil and swirl to coat. Add the garlic and mushrooms and stir-fry for 1 minute, or until soft. Add the spring onion, water chestnuts, baby corn and prawns. Cook for 2 minutes, or until the corn is just tender and the prawns begin to turn pink. Remove from the heat.

Carefully unroll the rice noodle roll and cut it in half. You need two 24 cm x 16 cm rectangles. Place 1/4 cup of the prawn mixture along one short end of each rectangle, leaving a 3 cm border. Fold both sides of the noodle roll towards the centre, then roll up like a spring roll. Cover with a damp tea towel and repeat with the remaining noodle rolls and prawn mixture.

Line a bamboo steamer with baking paper, brush with a little oil, then place the rolls in, seam-side-down. Place the steamer over a wok filled with simmering water and steam for 4–5 minutes, or until the prawns are cooked through.

Meanwhile, place the soy sauce, sesame oil, ginger, sugar and rice wine in a small saucepan and stir over medium heat to warm through. Place the rolls on a platter and drizzle with the sauce just before serving.

Serves 4

Udon noodle stir-fry with miso dressing

1 tablespoon white miso
1 tablespoon Japanese soy sauce
2 tablespoons sake
½ teaspoon sugar
400 g fresh udon noodles
1 tablespoon peanut oil
5 spring onions, cut into 5 cm lengths
1 red capsicum (pepper), thinly sliced
100 g fresh shiitake mushrooms, sliced
150 g snow peas (mangetout), sliced lengthways into strips

Combine the miso with the soy sauce to form a smooth paste. Add the sake and sugar and mix well.

Cook the udon noodles in a large saucepan of boiling salted water for 1–2 minutes, or until tender and plump. Drain and rinse under cold water.

Heat the oil in a wok over high heat and swirl to coat. Add the spring onion and capsicum and toss frequently for 1–2 minutes, or until softened slightly. Add the mushrooms and snow peas and stir-fry for 2–3 minutes, or until tender.

Add the noodles and miso mixture to the wok and toss until well combined. Serve immediately.

Serves 4

Noodle tempura with wasabi dressing

Wasabi dressing
½ teaspoon wasabi paste
1½ tablespoons Japanese soy sauce
3 tablespoons mirin

80 g dried ramen noodles
1 carrot, grated
2 nori sheets, shredded
2 spring onions, finely sliced
1¼ cups (155 g) tempura flour
1 cup (250 ml) iced water
oil, for deep-frying

Mix the wasabi paste and a little of the soy sauce to make a smooth paste. Add the mirin and remaining soy sauce and stir until there are no lumps.

Cook the noodles in a large saucepan of boiling salted water for 5 minutes, or until tender. Drain and rinse under cold water. Cut into 5 cm lengths with scissors. Transfer to a bowl. Mix in the carrot, nori and spring onion. Chill.

Place the tempura flour in a large bowl and make a well in the centre. Pour in the iced water and stir gently with chopsticks or a fork, until the flour and water are just combined (the batter should still be a little lumpy).

Fill a wok one-third full of oil and heat to 180°C (350°F), or until a cube of bread dropped into the oil browns in 15 seconds. Combine the noodle mixture and tempura batter, tossing lightly. Spoon ¼ cup (60 ml) of the mixture into the oil and, using a fork or chopsticks, quickly and carefully spread the mixture out a little. Cook for 2–3 minutes, turning occasionally, or until golden and cooked through. Remove and drain. Keep warm in a slow oven while you repeat with the remaining mixture. Serve immediately with the wasabi dressing.

Serves 4

Chinese omelettes with mushroom sauce

6 whole dried Chinese mushrooms
6 eggs, lightly beaten
4 spring onions, thinly sliced
1 small red capsicum (pepper),
 thinly sliced
1 cup (90 g) bean sprouts
2 teaspoons sesame oil
1 teaspoon soy sauce
1 tablespoon oil
1½ tablespoons oil, extra
2 cloves garlic, crushed
1 cup (250 ml) chicken stock
1 tablespoon oyster sauce
2 teaspoons soy sauce
1 teaspoon sugar
2 spring onions, sliced diagonally,
 extra
2 teaspoons cornflour

Place the mushrooms in a heatproof bowl, cover with boiling water and soak for 15 minutes. Drain, discard the stems and thinly slice the caps.

Meanwhile, mix the egg, spring onion, capsicum, bean sprouts, sesame oil and soy sauce in a bowl. Season.

Heat a wok over high heat, add 2 teaspoons oil and swirl to coat. Add a quarter of the egg mixture to the wok, swirl to coat evenly and cook for 1–2 minutes, or until almost set. Turn over and cook for 1 minute, or until brown. Remove and keep warm. Repeat with the remaining mixture, adding more oil if necessary.

Reheat the wok over high heat, add the extra oil and swirl. Add the garlic and mushrooms and cook for 1 minute. Add the stock, oyster sauce, soy sauce, sugar and extra spring onion. Bring to the boil, then reduce the heat and simmer for 1 minute. Combine the cornflour with 1 tablespoon water, add to the wok and simmer for 2 minutes, or until thickened slightly. Serve the omelettes topped with the sauce.

Serves 2–4

Stir-fried lamb with mint, chilli and Shanghai noodles

400 g Shanghai noodles
1 teaspoon sesame oil
2 tablespoons peanut oil
220 g lamb fillet, cut into thin strips
2 cloves garlic, crushed
2 fresh red chillies, seeded and
  finely sliced
1 tablespoon oyster sauce
2 teaspoons palm sugar
2 tablespoons fish sauce
2 tablespoons lime juice
½ cup (10 g) fresh mint, chopped
lime wedges, to garnish

Cook the noodles in a large saucepan of boiling water for 4–5 minutes. Drain, then rinse in cold water. Add the sesame oil and toss through.

Heat the peanut oil in a wok over high heat. Add the lamb and cook in batches for 1–2 minutes, or until just browned. Return all the meat to the wok and add the garlic and chilli. Cook for 30 seconds then add the oyster sauce, palm sugar, fish sauce, lime juice and noodles. Cook for another 2–3 minutes, or until the noodles are warm. Stir in the mint and serve immediately with the lime wedges.

Serves 4–6

Chinese beef and asparagus with oyster sauce

500 g lean beef fillet, thinly sliced
across the grain
1 tablespoon light soy sauce
1/2 teaspoon sesame oil
1 tablespoon Chinese rice wine
2 1/2 tablespoons vegetable oil
200 g fresh thin asparagus, cut into
thirds on the diagonal
3 cloves garlic, crushed
2 teaspoons julienned fresh ginger
1/4 cup (60 ml) chicken stock
2–3 tablespoons oyster sauce

Place the beef slices in a non-metallic bowl with the soy sauce, sesame oil and 2 teaspoons of the rice wine. Cover and marinate for at least 15 minutes.

Heat a wok over high heat, add 1 tablespoon of the vegetable oil and swirl to coat the side of the wok. When the oil is hot but not smoking, add the asparagus and stir-fry for 1–2 minutes. Remove from the wok.

Add another tablespoon of oil to the wok and, when hot, add the beef in two batches, stir-frying each batch for 1–2 minutes, or until cooked. Remove the meat from the wok.

Add the remaining oil to the wok and, when hot, add the garlic and ginger and stir-fry for 1 minute, or until fragrant. Pour the stock, oyster sauce and remaining rice wine into the wok, bring to the boil and boil rapidly for 1–2 minutes, or until the sauce is slightly reduced. Return the beef and asparagus to the wok and stir-fry for a further minute, or until heated through and coated in the sauce. Serve immediately with steamed rice.

Serves 4

Satay chicken stir-fry

1½ cups (300 g) jasmine rice
1½ tablespoons peanut oil
6 spring onions, cut into 3 cm lengths
800 g chicken breast fillets, thinly
  sliced on the diagonal
1–1½ tablespoons Thai red
  curry paste
⅓ cup (90 g) crunchy peanut butter
270 ml coconut milk
2 teaspoons soft brown sugar
1½ tablespoons lime juice

Bring a large saucepan of water to the boil. Add the rice and cook for 12 minutes, stirring occasionally. Drain well.

Meanwhile, heat a wok until very hot, add 1 teaspoon of the peanut oil and swirl to coat. When hot, add the spring onion and stir-fry for 30 seconds, or until softened slightly. Remove from the wok. Add a little extra peanut oil to the wok as needed and stir-fry the chicken in three batches for about 1 minute per batch, or until the meat just changes colour. Remove from the wok.

Add a little more oil to the wok, add the curry paste and stir-fry for 1 minute, or until fragrant. Add the peanut butter, coconut milk, sugar and 1 cup (250 ml) water and stir well. Bring to the boil and boil for 3–4 minutes, or until thickened and the oil starts to separate — reduce the heat slightly if the sauce spits at you. Return the chicken and the spring onion to the wok, stir well and cook for 2 minutes, or until heated through. Stir in the lime juice and season. Serve at once with the rice and a crisp green salad.

Serves 4

Squid with green peppercorns

600 g squid tubes
2 teaspoons chopped fresh
  coriander root
3 cloves garlic, crushed
4 tablespoons oil
25 g Thai green peppercorns on
  the stalk, in brine, or lightly
  crushed fresh peppercorns
2 tablespoons Thai mushroom
  soy sauce
1/2 teaspoon grated palm sugar
2/3 cup (20 g) fresh Thai basil
green peppercorns, extra,
  to garnish

Cut the squid tubes in half
lengthways. Cut a crisscross pattern
on the inside of the squid. Cut into
4 cm square pieces.

Place the coriander root, 1 clove
garlic and 1 tablespoon oil in a food
processor and process to form a
smooth paste. Mix together the paste
and squid pieces, cover and leave to
marinate for 30 minutes.

Heat a wok over high heat, add the
remaining oil and swirl to coat the
side. Add the squid pieces and
the remaining garlic and stir-fry for
1 minute. Add the peppercorns and
stir-fry for another 2 minutes, or until
the squid is just cooked — it will
toughen if overcooked. Add the soy
sauce and palm sugar, and stir until
the sugar has dissolved. Serve
immediately, garnished with Thai
basil and extra green peppercorns.

Serves 4

Note: Although the squid takes a
while to marinate, the actual time you
are kept in the kitchen is not long.

Grill

Tuna steaks on coriander noodles

¼ cup (60 ml) lime juice
2 tablespoons fish sauce
2 tablespoons sweet chilli sauce
2 teaspoons grated palm sugar
1 teaspoon sesame oil
1 clove garlic, finely chopped
1 tablespoon virgin olive oil
4 tuna steaks (150 g each), at
  room temperature
200 g dried thin wheat noodles
6 spring onions, thinly sliced
¾ cup (25 g) chopped fresh
  coriander leaves
lime wedges, to garnish

To make the dressing, place the lime juice, fish sauce, chilli sauce, sugar, sesame oil and garlic in a small bowl and mix together.

Heat the olive oil in a chargrill pan. Add the tuna steaks and cook over high heat for 2 minutes each side, or until cooked to your liking. Transfer the steaks to a warm plate, cover and keep warm.

Place the noodles in a large saucepan of lightly salted, rapidly boiling water and return to the boil. Cook for 4 minutes, or until the noodles are tender. Drain well. Add half the dressing and half the spring onion and coriander to the noodles and gently toss together.

Either cut the tuna into even cubes or slice it.

Place the noodles on serving plates and top with the tuna. Mix the remaining dressing with the spring onion and coriander and drizzle over the tuna. Garnish with lime wedges.

Serves 4

Note: If you prefer, you can serve the tuna steaks whole rather than cutting them into cubes. If serving whole, they would look better served with the noodles on the side.

Barbecued chermoula prawns

1 kg raw medium prawns
3 teaspoons hot paprika
2 teaspoons ground cumin
1 cup (30 g) firmly packed fresh
  flat-leaf parsley
½ cup (15 g) firmly packed fresh
  coriander leaves
100 ml lemon juice
145 ml olive oil
1½ cups (280 g) couscous
1 tablespoon grated lemon rind
lemon wedges, to serve

Peel the prawns, leaving the tails intact. Gently pull out the dark vein from the backs, starting at the head end. Place the prawns in a large bowl. Dry-fry the paprika and cumin in a frying pan for about 1 minute, or until fragrant. Remove from the heat.

Blend or process the spices, parsley, coriander, lemon juice and ½ cup (125 ml) of the oil until finely chopped. Add a little salt and pepper. Pour over the prawns and mix well, then cover with plastic wrap and refrigerate for 10 minutes. Heat a chargrill pan or barbecue plate to hot.

Meanwhile, to cook the couscous, bring 1 cup (250 ml) water to the boil in a saucepan, then stir in the couscous, lemon rind, the remaining oil and ¼ teaspoon salt. Remove from the heat, cover and leave for 5 minutes. Fluff the couscous with a fork, adding a little extra olive oil if needed.

Cook the prawns on the chargrill pan for about 3–4 minutes, or until cooked through, turning and brushing with extra marinade while cooking (take care not to overcook). Serve the prawns on a bed of couscous, with a wedge of lemon.

Serves 4

Paprika lamb kebabs with skordalia

1 kg lamb backstraps or eye of loin
  fillets, cut into 2 cm cubes
1 tablespoon sweet paprika
1 tablespoon hot paprika
½ cup (125 ml) lemon juice
½ cup (125 ml) olive oil
3 large (750 g) floury potatoes
  (e.g. russet), cut into large cubes
3–4 cloves garlic, crushed with
  a pinch of salt
300 g English spinach leaves
lemon wedges, to serve

Soak 12 wooden skewers in water for 30 minutes. Thread six lamb cubes onto each, then place in a non-metallic rectangular dish large enough to hold all the skewers in one layer.

Combine the paprikas, ⅓ cup (80 ml) lemon juice and ¼ cup (60 ml) oil in a small non-metallic jug. Pour over the skewers. Season. Cover and refrigerate.

For the skordalia, boil the potatoes for 20 minutes, or until tender. Drain and put in a food processor with the garlic and 1 tablespoon of the lemon juice. With the motor running, slowly add the remaining oil in a thin stream and continue blending for 30–60 seconds, or until all the oil is incorporated— avoid overprocessing as it will become gluey. Season. Set aside to serve at room temperature.

Heat a chargrill pan or barbecue plate and brush with oil. Cook the skewers for 3–4 minutes each side for medium-rare, or 5–6 minutes for well done.

Wash the spinach and add to a pan with just the water clinging to the leaves. Cook, covered, over medium heat for 1–2 minutes, or until wilted. Remove and stir in the remaining lemon juice. Serve the kebabs with skordalia, spinach and lemon wedges.

Serves 4

Grilled haloumi and roast vegetable salad

4 slender eggplants (aubergine), cut in half, halved lengthways
1 red capsicum (pepper), halved, thickly sliced
4 small zucchini (courgettes), cut in half, halved lengthways
⅓ cup (80 ml) olive oil
2 cloves garlic, crushed
200 g haloumi cheese, cut into 5 mm thick slices
150 g baby English spinach leaves, trimmed
1 tablespoon balsamic vinegar

Preheat the oven to hot 220°C (425°F/Gas 7). Place the vegetables in a large bowl, add ¼ cup (60 ml) olive oil and the garlic, season and toss well to combine. Place the vegetables in an ovenproof dish in a single layer and roast for 20–30 minutes, or until tender and browned around the edges.

Meanwhile, lightly brush a chargrill or heavy-based frying pan with oil and cook the haloumi slices for 1–2 minutes each side.

Place the spinach leaves on four serving plates. Top with the roast vegetables and haloumi. Place the remaining oil in a small jug, add the vinegar and whisk to combine, then pour over the vegetables and haloumi. Serve immediately, warm or at room temperature, with lots of crusty bread.

Serves 4

Note: You can use any roasted vegetable, such as orange sweet potatoes, leeks and Roma tomatoes.

Linguine with chargrilled basil and lemon seafood

16 raw medium prawns, peeled and deveined, with tails intact
350 g calamari rings
1/2 cup (125 ml) extra virgin olive oil
1/3 cup (80 ml) lemon juice
3 cloves garlic, crushed
1/2 teaspoon chilli flakes
3 tablespoons chopped fresh basil
400 g linguine
1 teaspoon grated lemon rind

Place the prawns and calamari in a non-metallic dish. To make the dressing, combine the olive oil and lemon juice in a small jug, then pour 1/4 cup (60 ml) into a small bowl, reserving the rest. Stir the garlic, chilli flakes and 2 tablespoons of the basil into the bowl, pour over the seafood and mix to coat well. Cover with plastic wrap and marinate in the refrigerator for 5–10 minutes.

Cook the pasta in a large saucepan of rapidly boiling salted water according to the packet instructions until *al dente*. Drain, then return to the pan.

Meanwhile, preheat a chargrill pan to high and brush with oil. Remove the prawns from the marinade with tongs and cook for 2–3 minutes each side, or until pink and cooked through. Remove. Add the calamari in batches and cook, turning once, for 1–3 minutes, or until opaque and cooked through—take care not to overcrowd the chargrill pan.

Transfer the pasta to a large serving bowl, then add the seafood, lemon rind and reserved dressing and gently toss together until the linguine is well coated. Garnish with the remaining basil and season to taste. Serve with a rocket salad.

Serves 4

White bean salad with tuna

1 cup (200 g) dried cannellini beans
or 1 x 425 g can cannellini beans,
rinsed and drained well
2 fresh bay leaves
1 large clove garlic, smashed
350 g green beans, trimmed
2 small baby fennel, thinly sliced
½ small red onion, very thinly sliced
1 cup (30 g) fresh flat-leaf parsley,
roughly chopped
1 tablespoon olive oil
2 fresh tuna steaks (400 g)
⅓ cup (80 ml) lemon juice
1 clove garlic, extra, finely chopped
1 small fresh red chilli, seeds removed,
finely chopped
1 teaspoon sugar
1 tablespoon lemon zest
½ cup (125 ml) extra virgin olive oil

Put the beans in a bowl, cover with cold water, allowing room for the beans to expand, and leave for at least 8 hours.

Rinse the beans well and transfer them to a saucepan. Cover with cold water, add the torn bay leaves and smashed garlic, and simmer for 20–25 minutes, or until tender. Drain.

Cook the green beans in boiling water for 1–2 minutes, or until tender, and refresh under cold water. Mix with the fennel, onion and parsley in a bowl.

Brush the oil over the tuna fillets and grill under high heat for 2 minutes on each side or until still pink in the centre. Remove, rest for 2–3 minutes, then cut into 3 cm chunks. Add to the green bean mixture and toss.

Mix the lemon juice, garlic, chilli, sugar and lemon zest together. Whisk in the extra virgin olive oil and season with salt and pepper. Toss gently through the salad.

Serves 4–6

Chargrilled vegetable salad with balsamic dressing

4 baby eggplants (aubergine)
5 Roma tomatoes
2 red capsicums (peppers)
1 green capsicum (pepper)
2 zucchini (courgettes)
100 ml olive oil
12 baby bocconcini
¼ cup (45 g) Ligurian olives
1 clove garlic, finely chopped
3 teaspoons baby capers
½ teaspoon sugar
2 tablespoons balsamic vinegar

Cut the eggplants and tomatoes in half lengthways. Cut the red and green capsicums in half lengthways, remove the seeds and membrane then cut each half into 3 pieces. Thinly slice the zucchini on the diagonal.

Preheat a chargrill pan. Add 1 tablespoon of oil and cook a quarter of the vegetables (cook the tomatoes cut-side down first) for about 2–3 minutes, or until marked and golden. Place in a bowl.

Cook the remaining vegetables in batches until tender, adding more oil as needed. Transfer to the bowl and add the baby bocconcini. Mix the olives, garlic, capers, sugar, vinegar and remaining oil (about 2 tablespoons). Pour over the salad and toss. Season with pepper.

Serves 4–6

Lamb cutlets with mint gremolata

4 tablespoons fresh mint leaves
1 tablespoon fresh flat-leaf parsley
2 cloves garlic
1½ tablespoons lemon rind (white
    pith removed), cut into thin strips
2 tablespoons extra virgin olive oil
8 French-trimmed lamb cutlets
2 carrots
2 zucchini (courgettes)
1 tablespoon lemon juice

To make the gremolata, finely chop the mint, parsley, garlic and lemon strips, then combine well.

Heat a chargrill pan or barbecue plate to very hot. Lightly brush with 1 tablespoon of the oil. Cook the cutlets over medium heat for 2 minutes on each side, or until cooked to your liking. Remove the cutlets and cover to keep warm.

Trim the ends from the carrots and zucchini and, using a sharp vegetable peeler, peel the vegetables lengthways into ribbons. Heat the remaining oil in a large saucepan, add the vegetables and toss over medium heat for 3–5 minutes, or until sautéed but tender.

Divide the cutlets among the serving plates, sprinkle the cutlets with the gremolata and drizzle with the lemon juice. Serve with the vegetable ribbons.

Serves 4

Vegetable skewers with basil couscous

5 thin zucchini (courgettes), cut into
2 cm cubes
5 slender eggplants (aubergine), cut
into 2 cm cubes
12 button mushrooms, halved
2 red capsicums (peppers), cut into
1.5 cm cubes
250 g kefalotyri cheese, cut into
2 cm thick pieces
1/3 cup (80 ml) lemon juice
2 garlic cloves, finely chopped
5 tablespoons finely chopped
fresh basil
145 ml extra virgin olive oil
1 cup (185 g) couscous
1 teaspoon grated lemon rind

Soak 12 wooden skewers in water for
30 minutes. Thread alternate pieces
of vegetables and kefalotyri, starting
and finishing with a piece of capsicum
and using two pieces of kefalotyri per
skewer. Place in a non-metallic dish
which will hold them in one layer.

Combine the lemon juice, garlic,
4 tablespoons basil and 1/2 cup (125 ml)
oil in a non-metallic bowl. Season.
Pour two thirds of the marinade over
the skewers, reserving the remainder.
Turn to coat, cover with plastic wrap
and marinate for at least 5 minutes.

Place the couscous, lemon rind and
1 1/2 cups (375 ml) boiling water in a
large heatproof bowl. Stand for
5 minutes, or until all the water has
been absorbed. Add the remaining oil
and basil, then fluff gently with a fork
to separate the grains. Cover.

Heat a chargrill pan or barbecue plate
to medium–high. Cook the skewers,
brushing often with the leftover
marinade, for 4–5 minutes on each
side, or until the vegetables are
cooked and the cheese browns.

Divide the couscous and skewers
among serving plates. Season, then
drizzle with the reserved marinade to
taste. Serve with lemon wedges.

Serves 4

Barbecued Asian pork ribs with spring onion rice

1 kg American-style pork ribs, cut into sections of 4–5 ribs
¼ cup (60 ml) hoisin sauce
1 tablespoon Chinese rice wine or dry sherry
¼ cup (60 ml) soy sauce
2 cloves garlic, chopped
2 tablespoons oil
3 spring onions, finely chopped
1 tablespoon grated fresh ginger
1¼ cups (250 g) jasmine rice
600 g baby bok choy, leaves separated

Place the ribs in a non-metallic bowl. Combine the hoisin sauce, rice wine, soy sauce, garlic, 1 tablespoon oil, 2 tablespoons spring onion and half the ginger. Pour over the ribs and marinate for at least 10 minutes, or overnight in the refrigerator.

Bring a large saucepan of water to the boil. Add the rice and cook for 12 minutes, stirring occasionally. Drain.

Heat the remaining oil in a small pan over medium–low heat. When the oil is warm but not smoking, remove the pan from the heat and add the rest of the spring onion and ginger. Stir in ¼ teaspoon salt. Stir through the rice.

Heat a chargrill pan or barbecue plate and brush with oil. Remove the ribs from the marinade, reserving the marinade. Cook the ribs in batches, if necessary, 8–10 minutes on each side, or until cooked through, basting with the marinade during cooking.

Before the ribs are cooked, bring the reserved marinade to the boil in a pan (add ⅓ cup/80 ml water if necessary). Boil for 2 minutes, then add the bok choy. Cover and cook for 1–2 minutes, or until just wilted. Serve the ribs with the rice and bok choy, and drizzle with the marinade.

Serves 4

Angel hair pasta with scallops and rocket

350 g angel hair pasta
100 g butter
3 cloves garlic, crushed
24 scallops, without roe
150 g baby rocket leaves
2 teaspoons finely grated lemon rind
¼ cup (60 ml) lemon juice
125 g semi-dried tomatoes,
  thinly sliced
30 g shaved Parmesan

Cook the pasta in a large saucepan of boiling water until *al dente*. Meanwhile, melt the butter in a small saucepan, add the garlic and cook over low heat, stirring, for 1 minute. Remove from the heat.

Heat a lightly greased chargrill plate over high heat and cook the scallops, brushing occasionally with some of the garlic butter for 1–2 minutes each side, or until cooked. Set aside and keep warm.

Drain the pasta and return to the pan with the remaining garlic butter, the rocket, lemon rind, lemon juice and tomato and toss until combined. Divide among four serving plates and top with the scallops. Season to taste and sprinkle with Parmesan.

Serves 4

Rosemary and red wine steaks with barbecued vegetables

12 small new potatoes
¼ cup (60 ml) olive oil
1 tablespoon finely chopped
   fresh rosemary
6 cloves garlic, sliced
sea salt flakes, to season
4 large, thick field mushrooms
12 asparagus spears
1 cup (250 ml) red wine
4 scotch fillet steaks
   (about 260 g each)

Heat a barbecue plate or chargrill pan to hot. Toss the potatoes with 1 tablespoon of the oil, half the rosemary and half the garlic and season with the sea salt flakes. Divide the potatoes among four large sheets of foil and wrap into neat packages, sealing firmly around the edges. Cook on the barbecue, turning frequently for 30–40 minutes, or until tender.

Meanwhile, brush the mushrooms and asparagus with a little of the remaining oil and set aside.

Combine the red wine with the remaining oil, rosemary and garlic in a non-metallic dish. Season with lots of freshly ground black pepper. Add the steaks and coat in the marinade. Allow to marinate for 25 minutes, then drain.

Cook the steaks and mushrooms on the barbecue for 4 minutes each side, or until cooked to your liking (this will depend on the thickness of the steak). Transfer the steaks and mushrooms to a plate, cover lightly and allow to rest. Add the asparagus to the barbecue, turning regularly for about 2 minutes, or until tender. Pierce the potatoes with a skewer to check for doneness. Season with salt and pepper. Serve the steaks with the vegetables.

Serves 4

Cajun chicken with fresh tomato and corn salsa

2 corn cobs
2 vine-ripened tomatoes, diced
1 Lebanese cucumber, diced
2 tablespoons roughly chopped
   fresh coriander leaves
4 chicken breast fillets
   (about 200 g each)
¼ cup (35 g) Cajun seasoning
2 tablespoons lime juice
lime wedges, to serve

Cook the corn cobs in a saucepan of boiling water for 5 minutes, or until tender. Remove the kernels using a sharp knife and place in a bowl with the tomato, cucumber and coriander. Season and mix well.

Heat a chargrill pan or barbecue plate to medium heat and brush lightly with oil. Pound each chicken breast between two sheets of plastic wrap with a mallet or rolling pin until 2 cm thick. Lightly coat the chicken with the Cajun seasoning and shake off any excess. Cook for 5 minutes on each side, or until just cooked through.

Just before serving, stir the lime juice into the salsa. Place a chicken breast on each plate and spoon the salsa on the side. Serve with the lime wedges, a green salad and crusty bread.

Serves 4

Sumac-crusted lamb fillets with baba ganouj

2 tablespoons olive oil
750 g small new potatoes
2–3 cloves garlic, crushed
cup (60 ml) lemon juice
1 red capsicum (pepper), seeded and quartered lengthways
4 lamb backstraps or eye of loin fillets (about 200 g each)
1 tablespoon sumac (see Note)
3 tablespoons finely chopped fresh flat-leaf parsely
250 g good-quality baba ganouj (eggplant/aubergine dip)

Heat the oil in a saucepan big enough to hold the potatoes in one layer. Cook the potatoes and garlic, turning frequently, for 3–5 minutes, or until golden. Add the lemon juice and reduce the heat to medium–low. Simmer, covered, for 15–20 minutes, or until tender, stirring occasionally. Season well.

Meanwhile, lightly oil a chargrill pan or barbecue plate and heat to very hot. Cook the capsicum skin-side-down for 1–2 minutes, or until the skin starts to blister and turn black. Cook the other side for 1–2 minutes. Place the capsicum in a plastic bag or bowl covered with plastic wrap.

Coat the lamb with sumac. Cook on the chargrill pan for 4–5 minutes each side, or until cooked to your liking. Remove and cover with foil. Peel the capsicum and slice into thin strips.

Stir the parsley through the potatoes. Divide the baba ganouj among four plates. Cut the lamb into 1 cm slices on the diagonal and arrange on the baba ganouj with the capsicum. Serve with the potatoes and a salad.

Serves 4

Note: Sumac is available from Middle Eastern food stores. If unavailable, use the same amount of ground cumin.

Gnocchi with creamy gorgonzola and sage sauce

2 x 500 g packets potato gnocchi
60 g butter
2 cloves garlic, crushed
½ cup (10 g) fresh small sage leaves
100 g gorgonzola cheese
150 ml cream
1 cup (100 g) grated Parmesan

Preheat the grill to high. Lightly grease four 1 cup (250 ml) heatproof gratin dishes. Cook the gnocchi in a large saucepan of rapidly boiling salted water according to the packet instructions until *al dente*. Lift the gnocchi out with a slotted spoon, leave to drain, then divide among the prepared dishes.

Melt the butter in a small saucepan over medium heat, add the garlic and sage leaves and cook for a few minutes, or until the leaves start to crispen and the garlic browns a little. Pour the sage butter evenly over the gnocchi in the gratin dishes.

Dot small knobs of the gorgonzola evenly among the gnocchi. Pour the cream over the top of each dish and sprinkle with the Parmesan. Place the dishes under the grill and cook until the top starts to brown and the gnocchi are heated through. Serve with a fresh green salad.

Serves 4

Note: This can also be cooked in a 1 litre rectangular heatproof ceramic dish or round pie dish.

Thai beef skewers with peanut sauce

1 onion, chopped
2 cloves garlic, crushed
2 teaspoons sambal oelek
1 stem lemon grass, white part only, chopped
2 teaspoons chopped fresh ginger
1½ tablespoons oil
270 ml coconut cream
½ cup (125 g) crunchy peanut butter
1½ tablespoons fish sauce
2 teaspoons soy sauce
1 tablespoon grated palm sugar or soft brown sugar
2 tablespoons lime juice
2 tablespoons chopped fresh coriander leaves
750 g round or rump steak, cut into 2 cm x 10 cm pieces
2 teaspoons oil, extra
fresh red chilli, chopped, to garnish (optional)
chopped roasted peanuts, to garnish (optional)

Put the onion, garlic, sambal oelek, lemon grass and ginger in a food processor and process to a smooth paste.

Heat the oil in a saucepan over medium heat, add the paste and cook, stirring, for 2–3 minutes, or until fragrant. Add the coconut cream, peanut butter, fish sauce, soy sauce, sugar and lime juice and bring to the boil. Reduce the heat and simmer for 5 minutes, then stir in the coriander.

Meanwhile, thread the meat onto 12 metal skewers, and cook on a hot chargrill or in a non-stick frying pan with the extra oil for 2 minutes each side, or until cooked to your liking. Serve the skewers on a bed of rice with the sauce and a salad on the side. Garnish with chopped chilli and peanuts, if desired.

Serves 4

Note: If using wooden skewers, soak them for 30 minutes before grilling to prevent them from burning.

Lime and coriander chargrilled chicken

3 teaspoons finely grated fresh ginger
½ cup (25 g) chopped fresh coriander
　leaves
1½ teaspoons grated lime rind
⅓ cup (80 ml) lime juice
4 skinless chicken breast fillets
　(about 750 g), trimmed
1¼ cups (250 g) jasmine rice
2 tablespoons oil
3 zucchini (courgettes), cut into
　wedges
4 large flat mushrooms,
　stalks trimmed

Combine the ginger, coriander, lime rind and 2 tablespoons of the lime juice. Spread 2 teaspoons of the herb mixture over each fillet and season well. Marinate for 1 hour. Combine the remaining herb mixture with the remaining lime juice in a screwtop jar. Set aside until needed.

Bring a large saucepan of water to the boil. Add the rice and cook for 12 minutes, stirring occasionally. Drain well.

Meanwhile, heat a chargrill pan or barbecue plate to medium—this will take about 5 minutes and lightly brush with oil. Brush the zucchini and mushrooms with the remaining oil. Place the chicken on the chargrill and cook on each side for 4–5 minutes, or until cooked through. Add the vegetables during the last 5 minutes of cooking, and turn frequently until browned on the outside and just softened. Cover with foil until ready to serve.

Divide the rice among four serving bowls. Cut the chicken fillets into long thick strips, then arrange on top of the rice. Shake the dressing well and drizzle over the chicken and serve with the chargrilled vegetables.

Serves 4

Chargrilled jumbo prawns

8 large raw king prawns (800 g)
⅓ cup (80 ml) olive oil
3 cloves garlic, crushed
1 tablespoon sweet chilli sauce
2 tablespoons lime juice
¼ cup (60 ml) olive oil, extra
2 tablespoons lime juice, extra
mixed lettuce leaves, to serve

Remove the heads from the prawns and, using a sharp knife, cut through the centre of the prawns lengthways to form two halves, leaving the tails and shells intact.

Place the olive oil, 2 crushed garlic cloves, sweet chilli sauce and lime juice in a large bowl, and mix together well. Add the prawns, toss to coat and marinate for 30 minutes.

Meanwhile, combine the extra oil and lime juice and remaining garlic in a bowl. Heat a barbecue or chargrill plate until hot. Drain the prawns and cook cut-side-down first, brushing with the marinade, for 1–2 minutes each side, or until cooked. Divide the lettuce among four serving plates, place the prawns on top and spoon over the dressing. Season and serve.

Serves 4

Grill

Barbecued steak with caramelised balsamic onions and mustard crème fraîche

1½ tablespoons wholegrain mustard
200 g crème fraîche
2 capsicums (peppers), 1 red and 1
  yellow, seeded and quartered
2 zucchini (courgettes), trimmed and
  sliced lengthways into strips
2 tablespoons oil
2 large red onions, thinly sliced
4 rump steaks (about 200 g each)
2 tablespoons soft brown sugar
¼ cup (60 ml) balsamic vinegar

Heat a barbecue hotplate or large chargrill pan to hot. Combine the mustard and crème fraîche in a bowl. Season. Cover and set aside.

Brush the capsicum and zucchini with 1 tablespoon oil. Cook the capsicum, turning regularly, for 5 minutes, or until tender and slightly charred. Remove and cover with foil. Repeat with the zucchini, cooking for 5 minutes.

Heat the remaining oil on the hotplate, then cook the onion, turning occasionally, for 5–10 minutes, or until softened. When nearly soft, push to the side of the hotplate, then add the steaks and cook on each side for 3–4 minutes (medium-rare), or until cooked to your liking. Remove the steaks, cover with foil and allow to rest. Spread the onion over the hotplate once again, reduce the heat, sprinkle with sugar and cook for 1–2 minutes, or until the sugar has dissolved and the onion appears glossy. Add the vinegar, stirring continuously for 1–2 minutes, or until it is absorbed. Remove at once.

Peel the capsicum, then divide among serving plates with the zucchini. Place the steaks on top, season and top with the balsamic onions. Serve with the mustard crème fraîche and a salad.

Serves 4

Stuffed mushrooms with spiced couscous

8 field mushrooms
1/2 cup (95 g) instant couscous
1 tablespoon extra virgin olive oil
1 teaspoon ground cumin
1/4 teaspoon cayenne pepper
2 teaspoons finely grated lemon rind
1/2 cup (125 ml) chicken stock
1 tomato, finely chopped
1 tablespoon lemon juice
2 tablespoons chopped fresh
   flat-leaf parsley
2 tablespoons chopped fresh mint

Peel the mushrooms and remove the stalks, then grill them top-side up.

Place the couscous, olive oil, cumin, cayenne pepper and lemon rind in a bowl. Season, then stir the flavourings through the couscous.

Bring the chicken stock to the boil and stir it into the couscous. Cover and leave for 5 minutes, then fluff the grains with a fork. Stir in the tomato, lemon juice, parsley and mint. Fill each mushroom with some of the couscous mixture and pack down firmly. Grill until the couscous is golden. Serve hot or cold.

Makes 8

Tandoori chicken with cardamom rice

200 g plain yoghurt, plus extra
  for serving
¼ cup (60 g) good-quality tandoori
  paste
2 tablespoons lemon juice
1 kg chicken breast fillets, cut into
  3 cm cubes
1 tablespoon oil
1 onion, finely diced
1½ cups (300 g) long-grain rice
2 cardamom pods, bruised
3 cups (750 ml) hot chicken stock
400 g English spinach leaves

Soak eight wooden skewers in water for 30 minutes to prevent them burning during cooking. Combine the yoghurt, tandoori paste and lemon juice in a non-metallic dish. Add the chicken and coat well, then cover and marinate for at least 10 minutes.

Meanwhile, heat the oil in a saucepan. Add the onion and cook for 3 minutes, then add the rice and cardamom pods. Cook, stirring often, for 3–5 minutes, or until the rice is slightly opaque. Add the stock and bring to the boil. Reduce the heat to low, cover, and cook, without removing the lid, for 15 minutes.

Heat a barbecue plate or oven grill to very hot. Thread the chicken cubes onto the skewers, leaving the bottom quarter of the skewers empty. Cook on each side for 4–5 minutes, or until cooked through.

Wash the spinach and place in a large saucepan with just the water clinging to the leaves. Cook, covered, over medium heat for 1–2 minutes, or until the spinach has wilted. Uncover the rice, fluff with a fork and serve with the spinach, chicken and extra yoghurt.

Serves 4

Lamb pide with garlic and chickpea purée

1 tablespoon lemon juice
1 teaspoon ground cumin
1 tablespoon olive oil
4 trimmed lamb fillets
1 bulb of garlic
½ cup (100 g) canned chickpeas,
    drained
2 teaspoons lemon juice, extra
1 tablespoon low-fat plain yoghurt
4 x 100 g pieces Turkish bread

Mix the lemon juice, cumin, olive oil and some salt and pepper. Add the lamb fillets and leave to marinate for at least 1 hour.

Preheat the oven to hot 210°C (415°F/Gas 6–7). Wrap the bulb of garlic in foil, then roast for 20 minutes, or until soft. Cool, then squeeze out the pulp from each clove. Purée the pulp with the chickpeas, extra lemon juice and low-fat yoghurt in a food processor—add a little water to achieve a spreading consistency, if needed. Season.

Grill or barbecue the lamb for 3 minutes on each side, or until done to your liking. Grill or toast the Turkish bread, then slice through the middle and spread with the chickpea spread. Top with thin slices of the lamb, tomato and rocket leaves.

Serves 4

Chargrilled baby octopus

1.5 kg baby octopus
1 cup (250 ml) sweet chilli sauce
⅓ cup (80 ml) lime juice
⅓ cup (80 ml) fish sauce
⅓ cup (60 g) soft brown sugar
oil, for chargrilling
200 g mixed salad leaves, to serve
lime wedges, to serve

Cut the head from the octopus and discard. With your fingers, push the hard beak up and out of the body. Rinse, drain and pat dry.

Place the sweet chilli sauce, lime juice, fish sauce and sugar in a small bowl and mix together well.

Brush a chargrill plate or barbecue with oil and heat to very hot. Cook the octopus, turning, for 3–4 minutes, or until they change colour. Brush with a quarter of the sauce during cooking. Do not overcook. Serve immediately on a bed of salad greens with the remaining sauce and the lime wedges.

Serves 4

Oven

Polenta with mushrooms, spinach and tomatoes

4 Roma tomatoes, halved lengthways
4 large field mushrooms
1/3 cup (80 ml) garlic-flavoured oil
(see Note)
900 ml vegetable stock
175 g instant polenta
150 g goat's cheese, chopped
1/2 cup (50 g) grated Parmesan
300 g baby English spinach leaves

Place the tomato and mushrooms in a non-metallic dish, brush with half the garlic oil, and leave to marinate for 30 minutes. Preheat the oven to moderately hot 200°C (400°F/Gas 6).

Place the tomato in a baking dish and bake for 20 minutes. Meanwhile, place the stock in a large saucepan and bring to the boil, add the polenta in a slow steady stream and cook, stirring, for 10 minutes, or until creamy. Stir in the goat's cheese and half the Parmesan. Remove from the heat and keep warm.

Heat 1 tablespoon garlic oil in a frying pan, add the mushrooms and cook, turning once, for 3–4 minutes, or until cooked, but not starting to release too much juice. Remove from the pan. Add the remaining oil to the pan, add the spinach and cook for 3–4 minutes, or until just wilted. Spoon the polenta onto four warm serving plates, arrange the spinach on top, then a mushroom and top with two tomato halves. Sprinkle with the remaining Parmesan and serve.

Serves 4

Note: Garlic-flavoured oil is available at delicatessens. Or, marinate a crushed garlic clove in 1/3 cup (80 ml) virgin olive oil for 2 hours, then strain.

Rustic Greek pie

450 g packet frozen spinach, thawed
1 large sheet ready-rolled shortcrust
  pastry, thawed
3 cloves garlic, finely chopped
150 g haloumi, grated
120 g feta, crumbled
1 tablespoon fresh oregano sprigs
2 eggs
¼ cup (60 ml) cream
lemon wedges, to serve

Preheat the oven to moderately hot
200°C (400°F/Gas 6). Squeeze the
excess liquid from the spinach.

Place the pastry on a baking tray and
spread the spinach in the middle,
leaving a 3 cm border around the
edge. Sprinkle the garlic over the
spinach and pile the haloumi and feta
on top. Sprinkle with oregano and
season well. Cut a short slit into each
corner of the pastry, then tuck each
side of pastry over to form a border
around the filling.

Lightly beat the eggs with the cream
and carefully pour the egg mixture
over the spinach filling. Bake for
25–30 minutes, or until the pastry
is golden and the filling is set. Serve
with the lemon wedges and a fresh
green salad.

Serves 4

Mushroom pot pies

100 ml olive oil
1 leek, sliced
1 clove garlic, crushed
1 kg field mushrooms,
  roughly chopped
1 teaspoon chopped fresh thyme
300 ml cream
1 sheet ready-rolled puff pastry,
  thawed
1 egg yolk, beaten, to glaze

Preheat the oven to moderate 180°C (350°F/Gas 4). Heat 1 tablespoon oil in a frying pan over medium heat. Cook the leek and garlic for 5 minutes, or until the leek is soft and translucent. Transfer to a large saucepan.

Heat the remaining oil in the frying pan over high heat and cook the mushrooms in two batches, stirring frequently, for 5–7 minutes per batch, or until the mushrooms have released their juices and are soft. Transfer to the saucepan, then add the thyme.

Place the saucepan over high heat and stir in the cream until well mixed. Cook, stirring occasionally, for 7–8 minutes, or until the cream has reduced to a thick sauce. Remove from the heat and season well.

Divide the filling among four 1¼ cup (315 ml) ramekins or ovenproof bowls. Cut the pastry into rounds slightly larger than each dish. Brush the rim of the ramekins with a little of the egg yolk, place the pastry on top and press down to seal. Brush the top with the remaining egg yolk. Place the ramekins on a metal tray. Bake for 20–25 minutes, or until the pastry has risen and is golden brown. Great with mashed potato and a salad.

Serves 4

Rack of lamb with mustard crust and parsley potatoes

2 racks of lamb (6 chops per rack), trimmed
1/4 cup (60 ml) oil
2 cups (160 g) fresh breadcrumbs
3 cloves garlic, chopped
1 teaspoon grated lemon rind
1/2 cup (10 g) fresh flat-leaf parsley, finely chopped
2 tablespoons tarragon Dijon mustard
150 g unsalted butter, softened
400 g baby new potatoes

Preheat the oven to hot 220°C (425°F/Gas 7). Score the fat side of the racks in a crisscross pattern. Rub 1 tablespoon of the oil over the racks and season well. Heat the remaining oil in a frying pan over medium heat and cook the racks for 5–8 minutes, or until the surface is completely brown. Remove from the pan.

Combine the breadcrumbs, garlic, lemon rind and three quarters of the parsley. Add the mustard and 100 g of the butter to form a paste. Firmly press a layer of breadcrumb mixture over the fat side of the racks, then place in a roasting tin. Bake for 25 minutes, or until the breadcrumbs appear brown and crisp and the meat is cooked to medium. For well-done, continue to bake for 10 minutes, or until cooked to your liking. Cover the breadcrumb crust with foil to prevent it burning, if necessary.

About 25 minutes before the lamb is ready, toss the potatoes with the remaining butter until well coated. Season, then put in a roasting tin. Bake for 20 minutes, or until brown, then remove, sprinkle with the remaining parsley and season. To serve, cut the racks in half using the bones as a guide. Serve with the pan juices, potatoes and a tossed salad.

Serves 4

Roasted vegetable cannelloni

60 g butter
1 large leek, cut into 1 cm pieces
200 g purchased chargrilled eggplant (aubergine) in oil
200 g purchased chargrilled orange sweet potato in oil
1 cup (125 g) firmly packed grated Cheddar
⅓ cup (40 g) plain flour
1 litre milk
6 fresh lasagne sheets

Preheat the oven to moderately hot 200°C (400°F/Gas 6) and lightly grease a ceramic dish (28 cm x 18 cm x 5 cm). Melt 20 g butter in a saucepan, add the leek and stir over medium heat for 8 minutes, or until soft. Chop the eggplant and sweet potato into 1 cm pieces and place in a bowl. Mix in the leek and ⅓ cup (40 g) of the Cheddar.

Melt the remaining butter in a saucepan over medium heat. Stir in the flour and cook for 1 minute, or until foaming. Remove from the heat and gradually stir in the milk. Return to the heat and stir until the sauce boils and thickens. Reduce the heat and simmer for 2 minutes. Season with salt and ground black pepper. Stir 1½ cups (375 ml) of the sauce into the vegetable mixture, adding extra if necessary to bind it together.

Cut the rectangular lasagne sheets in half widthways to make two smaller rectangles. Spoon vegetable mixture along the centre of one sheet and roll up. Repeat to make 12 tubes in total.

Place the tubes, seam-side-down, in the dish and spoon the remaining white sauce over the top until they are covered. Sprinkle with the remaining cheese and bake for about 20 minutes, or until the cheese is golden.

Serves 4

Chilli con carne

1 tablespoon oil
1 large red onion, finely chopped
2 cloves garlic, crushed
1½ teaspoons chilli powder
1 teaspoon ground oregano
2 teaspoons ground cumin
500 g lean beef mince
2 x 400 g cans chopped tomatoes
420 g can red kidney beans, drained
  and rinsed
8 flour tortillas
sour cream, to serve, optional

Preheat the oven to moderate 180°C (350°F/Gas 4). Heat the oil in a large saucepan, add the onion and garlic and cook, stirring, over medium heat for about 2–3 minutes, or until softened. Add the chilli powder, oregano and cumin and stir until fragrant. Add the mince and cook, stirring, for about 5 minutes, or until browned all over, breaking up any lumps with the back of a wooden spoon.

Add the tomato, beans and ½ cup (125 ml) water and simmer, stirring occasionally, for about 30 minutes, or until thick. Season to taste with salt and pepper. About 10 minutes before serving, wrap the tortillas in foil and heat them in the oven according to packet instructions to soften. Fill the tortillas with the chilli and wrap. Serve with sour cream and, if desired, a green salad.

Serves 4

Note: You can top jacket potatoes with chilli con carne and a dollop of sour cream, or serve it with rice.

Chicken casserole with mustard and tarragon

¼ cup (60 ml) olive oil
1 kg chicken thigh fillets, halved,
   then quartered
1 onion, finely chopped
1 leek, sliced
1 clove garlic, finely chopped
350 g button mushrooms, sliced
½ teaspoon dried tarragon
1½ cups (375 ml) chicken stock
¾ cup (185 ml) cream
2 teaspoons lemon juice
2 teaspoons Dijon mustard

Preheat the oven to moderate 180°C (350°F/ Gas 4). Heat 1 tablespoon of the oil in a flameproof casserole dish over medium heat, and cook the chicken in two batches for 6–7 minutes each, or until golden. Remove from the dish.

Add the remaining oil to the casserole dish and cook the onion, leek and garlic over medium heat for 5 minutes, or until soft. Add the mushrooms and cook for 5–7 minutes, or until they are soft and browned, and most of the liquid has evaporated. Add the tarragon, chicken stock, cream, lemon juice and mustard, bring to the boil and cook for 2 minutes. Return the chicken pieces to the dish and season well. Cover.

Place the casserole in the oven and cook for 1 hour, or until the sauce has reduced and thickened. Season to taste with salt and pepper, and serve with potatoes and a green salad.

Serves 4–6

Roast rack of pork with fig and Marsala sauce

300 g dessert figs, quartered
⅓ cup (80 ml) Marsala
2 teaspoons Dijon mustard
½ cup (125 ml) chicken stock
1.5 kg rack of pork, tied
120 ml oil
1 large red onion, sliced
18 fresh sage leaves
300 g beans, trimmed

Preheat the oven to very hot 240°C (475°F/Gas 9). Soak the figs, Marsala, mustard and stock for 30 minutes. Score the rind of the pork in lines 5 cm apart, brush with 2 tablespoons oil and season. Place in a large roasting tin, cook for 15 minutes, then reduce the heat to moderately hot 200°C (400°F/ Gas 6). Add the onion, bake for 40 minutes, then add the fig mixture and bake for 30–40 minutes, or until the pork juices run clear when the thickest section is pierced with a skewer.

Meanwhile, heat the remaining oil in a small saucepan over high heat. Add the sage leaves a few at a time for 30 seconds per batch. Remove with a slotted spoon and drain.

Remove the pork and onion pieces from the oven and allow the meat to rest for 5 minutes. Drain the excess fat from the roasting tin. Reduce the sauce on the stovetop for 5 minutes, stirring to scrape up any sediment stuck to the base of the pan.

Cook the beans in boiling water for 4 minutes. Drain, season. Keep warm.

Slice the pork into portions, pour on the sauce and garnish with the sage leaves. Serve with the onions, beans and, if desired, mashed potato.

Serves 4

Pumpkin tarts

6 sheets ready-rolled puff pastry
1.2 kg pumpkin, cut into 6 cm pieces
6 tablespoons sour cream or cream
  cheese
sweet chilli sauce, to serve

Preheat the oven to moderately hot 200°C (400°F/Gas 6). Lightly grease six 10 cm pie dishes. Cut six 15 cm circles from the pastry, carefully place in the prepared dishes and pleat the pastry to fit. Prick the pastry with a fork. Place on a baking tray and bake for 15–20 minutes, or until lightly golden, pressing down any pastry that puffs up. Cool.

Meanwhile, steam the pumpkin pieces for about 15 minutes, or until just tender.

Place a tablespoon of sour cream in the middle of each pastry shell and pile the pumpkin pieces on top. Season with salt and black pepper and drizzle with sweet chilli sauce to taste. Return to the oven for 5 minutes to heat through. Remove from the tins and serve immediately.

Serves 6

Aromatic snapper parcels

1 cup (30 g) loosely packed fresh
basil leaves, chopped
2 large cloves garlic, chopped
1 tablespoon lemon juice
1 teaspoon grated lemon rind
¼ cup (60 ml) olive oil
4 skinless snapper fillets, trimmed and
boned (about 200 g each)
500 g small new potatoes
20 asparagus spears
12 yellow baby squash

Preheat the oven to moderately hot
200°C (400°F/Gas 6). Combine the
basil, garlic, lemon juice, rind and
2 tablespoons of the olive oil. Season.

Place a fish fillet in the centre of a
sheet of foil large enough to fully
enclose it. Season. Smear the fillet
with 2 teaspoons of the basil mixture,
then wrap into a secure parcel with
the foil. Repeat with the remaining
fillets. Place on a baking tray and
refrigerate until required.

Cook the potatoes in a saucepan of
boiling water for 15–20 minutes, or
until tender. Drain and keep warm.
While the potatoes are cooking, brush
the asparagus and squash with the
remaining oil. Place on a baking tray
and season with freshly ground black
pepper. Bake for 8–10 minutes, or
until golden and tender.

About 10 minutes before the
vegetables are ready, place the fish
parcels in the oven and cook for
5–7 minutes, or until the flesh flakes
easily when tested with a fork. Check
one of the parcels after 5 minutes to
see if the fish is cooked through.
Place the opened parcels on serving
plates with the vegetables, season to
taste and serve.

Serves 4

Mustard-crusted scotch fillet with roast vegetables

16 French shallots
½ cup (125 g) wholegrain mustard
3 cloves garlic, crushed
1.2–1.5 kg scotch fillet
200 g parsnips, cut into 2 cm chunks
400 g potatoes, cut lengthways
    into wedges
200 g orange sweet potato, cut
    into wedges
⅓ cup (80 ml) olive oil

Preheat the oven to moderately hot 200°C (400°F/Gas 6). Peel four of the French shallots, slice into thick rings and arrange them in the centre of a large roasting tin.

Combine the mustard and garlic, and season well with salt and pepper. Rub the mixture over the surface of the beef, then place the beef on top of the sliced shallots. Toss the parsnip, potato, sweet potato, the remaining shallots, and ¼ cup (60 ml) of the oil together, then arrange around the beef. Drizzle the remaining oil over the beef and roast for 30 minutes.

Season and turn the vegetables— don't worry if some of the mustard mixes through. Roast for a further 30 minutes for a medium–rare result, or until cooked to your liking. Rest in a warm place for 10 minutes.

To serve, carve the beef and spoon the pan juices on the top. Serve with the roasted vegetables, whole shallots, and some steamed greens, if desired.

Serves 4

Moroccan roast lamb with mint couscous

2 tablespoons olive oil
3 teaspoons ground cumin
3 teaspoons ground coriander
3 teaspoons sweet paprika
3 cloves garlic, crushed
1.5 kg easy-carve leg of lamb
1⅓ cups (245 g) couscous
2 tablespoons chopped fresh mint

Preheat the oven to moderate 180°C (350°F/Gas 4). Combine the oil, spices and 2 cloves crushed garlic to form a smooth paste. Season with salt and pepper. Rub a thick coating of the paste all over the lamb. Place on a rack in a roasting tin and roast for 1 hour 15 minutes, basting two or three times. Allow to rest in a warm place for 10 minutes.

Meanwhile, place the couscous in a heatproof bowl with 2 cups (500 ml) boiling water. Stir in the mint, the remaining garlic and ½ teaspoon salt. Cover and leave for 5 minutes, or until all the water has been absorbed, then gently fluff with a fork.

To serve, carve the lamb into thick slices and place on a bed of couscous. Pour the pan juices into a small jug and serve with the lamb. Garnish with fresh mint leaves, if desired.

Serves 4

Note: The lamb is baked for a long time, but the rest of this recipe takes no effort so it is quick to prepare.

Baked ricotta with ratatouille

1.5 kg ricotta, well drained
4 eggs, lightly beaten
3 cloves garlic, finely chopped
2 tablespoons chopped fresh thyme
⅓ cup (80 ml) olive oil
300 g eggplant, diced
3 capsicums (peppers), green, red
and yellow, diced
425 g can crushed tomatoes

Preheat the oven to moderate 180°C (350°F/Gas 4). Place the ricotta, eggs, 1 finely chopped garlic clove and 1 tablespoon chopped fresh thyme in a bowl. Season and mix well. Pour the mixture into a lightly greased 22 cm springform pan and gently tap a couple of times on the bench to expel any air bubbles. Bake for 1 hour 30 minutes, or until firm and golden. Cool on a rack, pressing down from time to time to remove any air bubbles.

Meanwhile, heat 2 tablespoons oil in a frying pan, add the eggplant and cook for 4–5 minutes, or until golden. Add the capsicum and remaining garlic, and cook for 5 minutes, adding an extra tablespoon oil if necessary. Stir in the tomato and remaining thyme, and cook for 10–15 minutes, or until rich and pulpy. Season. Remove the ricotta from the springform pan and cut into wedges. Serve with a little ratatouille on the side, garnished with thyme sprigs.

Serves 8

Note: Although this recipe cooks for a long time, it is quick to prepare.

Balsamic roasted veal cutlets with red onion

1½ tablespoons olive oil
8 veal cutlets
4 cloves garlic, unpeeled
1 red onion, cut into thin wedges
1 tablespoon chopped fresh rosemary
250 g cherry tomatoes
¼ cup (60 ml) balsamic vinegar
2 teaspoons soft brown sugar
2 tablespoons chopped fresh
    flat-leaf parsley

Preheat the oven to moderately hot 200°C (400°F/Gas 6). Heat the oil in a large frying pan over medium heat. Cook the cutlets in batches for 4 minutes on both sides, or until brown.

Arrange the cutlets in a single layer in a large, shallow-sided roasting tin. Add the garlic, onion, rosemary, tomatoes, vinegar and sugar. Season well with salt and freshly ground black pepper.

Cover tightly with foil and roast for 15 minutes. Remove the foil and roast for another 10–15 minutes, depending on the thickness of the veal chops.

Transfer the cutlets, garlic, onion and tomatoes to serving plates. Stir the pan juices and spoon over the top. Garnish with the chopped parsley and serve immediately. Delicious with a creamy garlic mash and a tossed green salad.

Serves 4

Chicken, broccoli and pasta bake

300 g fusilli
425 g can cream of mushroom soup
2 eggs
3/4 cup (185 g) whole-egg mayonnaise
1 tablespoon Dijon mustard
1 2/3 cups (210 g) grated Cheddar
600 g chicken breast fillets,
  thinly sliced
400 g frozen broccoli pieces, thawed
1/2 cup (40 g) fresh breadcrumbs

Preheat the oven to moderate 180°C (350°F/Gas 4). Cook the pasta in a large saucepan of boiling water until *al dente*, then drain and return to the pan. Combine the soup, eggs, mayonnaise, mustard and half the cheese in a bowl.

Heat a lightly greased non-stick frying pan over medium heat, add the chicken pieces and cook for 5–6 minutes, or until cooked through. Season with salt and pepper, then set aside to cool.

Add the chicken and broccoli to the pasta, pour the soup mixture over the top and stir until well combined. Transfer the mixture to a 3-litre ovenproof dish. Sprinkle with the combined breadcrumbs and remaining cheese. Bake for 20 minutes, or until the top is golden brown.

Serves 6–8

Roast peppered beef with onions and potatoes

1 kg piece beef sirloin
2 tablespoons freshly ground black
    peppercorns
1 large red onion
4 large potatoes
50 g butter
¼ cup (60 ml) beef stock
¼ cup (60 ml) red wine
500 g mixed yellow and green beans

Preheat the oven to moderate 180°C (350°F/Gas 4). Trim the excess fat from the beef, leaving a thin layer. Press the pepper all over the beef.

Cut the onion and potatoes into 5 mm thick slices and place in a roasting tin. Sit the beef on top, fat-side-up. Cut 40 g of the butter into small pieces and dot all over the beef and potatoes. Pour in the stock and wine and bake for 35–40 minutes, for medium–rare, or until cooked to your liking. Remove the beef from the oven and rest for at least 5 minutes before carving.

Meanwhile, bring a saucepan of lightly salted water to the boil. Add the mixed beans and cook for 2–4 minutes, or until just tender. Drain well, then add the remaining butter and toss. Keep warm until ready to serve.

To serve, divide the onion and potato mixture among four serving plates and top with slices of beef. Spoon on any pan juices and serve with the beans.

Serves 4

Shepherd's pie with garlic mash

1½ tablespoons oil
1 large onion, finely chopped
1 carrot, finely diced
8 garlic cloves, peeled
750 g lean lamb mince
1½ cups (375 ml) Italian tomato
  pasta sauce
300 ml beef stock
800 g potatoes, cut into
  large chunks
30 g butter

Heat the oil in a large saucepan over medium heat. Add the onion and carrot and cook for 5 minutes, or until soft. Crush 2 garlic cloves and sauté with the onion for another minute. Add the lamb and stir well, breaking up any lumps with the back of a wooden spoon. Cook for 5 minutes, or until browned and cooked through. Spoon off any excess fat, then add the tomato pasta sauce and 1 cup (250 ml) stock. Cover and bring to the boil. Reduce the heat to medium–low and simmer for 25 minutes. Uncover and cook for 20 minutes, or until the sauce thickens. Preheat the oven to moderately hot 200°C (400°F/Gas 6).

Meanwhile, cook the potato in a pan of boiling water with the remaining garlic for 15–20 minutes, or until tender. Drain well, then return to the pan over low heat, stirring to evaporate any excess water. Remove from the heat, add the butter and the remaining stock and mash until smooth. Season.

Transfer the lamb mixture to a 1.5 litre ovenproof ceramic dish. Spread the potato over the top. Use a fork to swirl the surface. Bake for 40 minutes, or until the potato is golden brown.

Serves 4

Note: Shepherd's pie has a long cooking time but is quick to prepare.

Artichoke, olive and goat's cheese pizza

25 cm purchased pizza base
⅓ cup (80 ml) Italian tomato pasta
 sauce
150 g marinated artichokes,
 quartered
70 g pitted Kalamata olives
1 clove garlic, thinly sliced
50 g goat's cheese, crumbled
good-quality olive oil, to drizzle
2 tablespoons chopped fresh oregano

Preheat the oven to hot 220°C (425°F/Gas 7). Place the pizza base on a baking tray, then spread with the tomato pasta sauce. Evenly scatter the artichoke pieces, olives and the garlic over the pasta sauce, then top with the crumbled goat's cheese.

Lightly drizzle the surface of the pizza with olive oil and bake for 20 minutes, or until golden. Sprinkle with fresh oregano and season with salt and freshly ground black pepper. Cut into wedges and serve.

Serves 4

Lamb kofta curry

1¼ cups (250 g) jasmine rice
1 kg lean lamb mince
1 egg, lightly beaten
2 onions, finely chopped
120 g Korma curry paste
4 tablespoons chopped fresh
  coriander leaves
2 cloves garlic, crushed
2 tablespoons oil
400 g can diced tomatoes

Preheat the oven to hot 220°C (425°F/ Gas 7) and lightly grease two baking trays. Bring a large saucepan of water to the boil. Add the rice and cook for 12 minutes, stirring occasionally. Drain.

Meanwhile, combine the mince, egg, 1 onion, 2 tablespoons curry paste, 3 tablespoons coriander, 1 garlic clove and salt and form tablespoons of the mixture into balls. Place on one of the baking trays.

Heat 1 tablespoon oil in a large non-stick frying pan over medium heat. Cook the balls in batches for 1 minute on each side, or until evenly golden, but not cooked through. Place on the second tray and bake for 5–7 minutes, or until cooked through.

Wipe the pan clean. Heat the remaining oil over medium heat. Add the remaining onion and garlic and cook for 3 minutes, or until the onion is soft. Add the remaining curry paste, cook for 1 minute, then add the tomato and 1 cup (250 ml) water. Bring to the boil, then reduce the heat and simmer for 10 minutes, or until the sauce thickens slightly. Season. Stir the meatballs and their juices into the sauce. Simmer for 5 minutes to warm the meatballs. Serve with rice and sprinkle with coriander.

Serves 4

Mexican chicken bake

¾ cup (165 g) short-grain rice
300 g can red kidney beans,
   drained and thoroughly rinsed
3½ tablespoons chopped fresh
   coriander leaves
1 tablespoon oil
600 g skinless chicken thigh fillets,
   unrolled
2 x 200 g jars spicy taco sauce
2 cups (250 g) grated Cheddar
½ cup (125 g) sour cream

Preheat the oven to moderate 180°C
(350°F/Gas 4). Lightly grease a deep
(7 cm) round (21 cm) ceramic
casserole dish. Bring a large
saucepan of water to the boil, add
the rice and cook for 10–12 minutes,
stirring occasionally. Drain.

In the prepared dish, combine the
beans and 1½ tablespoons of the
coriander, then add the rice and toss
together. Lightly press the mixture so
the beans are mixed into the rice and
the mixture is flat.

Heat the oil in a large frying pan over
medium–high heat. Sauté the chicken
thighs for 3 minutes, then turn over.
Add the spicy taco sauce, and cook
for another 3 minutes.

To assemble, spread half the cheese
over the rice. Arrange the thighs and
sauce on top in a star shape, sprinkle
with 1½ tablespoons coriander, then
sprinkle with cheese. Cover with foil.

Bake for 35–40 minutes, or until the
mixture is bubbling and the cheese is
melted and slightly browned—remove
the foil for the last 5 minutes. Cut into
four servings with a knife and scoop
out carefully, keeping the layers intact.
Serve sprinkled with the remaining
coriander and a dollop of sour cream.

Serves 4

Pork loin roast with apple walnut stuffing and roast vegetables

½ cup (50 g) walnuts, chopped
1 green apple, peeled and cored
½ teaspoon ground cinnamon
2 tablespoons port
1.5 kg rindless, boned pork loin
100 ml maple syrup
8 parsnips, sliced thinly lengthways
500 g baby carrots
2 tablespoons oil

Preheat the oven to moderately hot 200°C (400°F/Gas 6). Grease a large roasting tin. Spread the walnuts on a baking tray and place under a medium–high grill for 2–3 minutes, or until lightly toasted.

Coarsely grate the apple and squeeze out the excess juice. Combine the apple, cinnamon, walnuts and port and season to taste.

Unroll the pork loin, then spread the stuffing evenly over one third of the loin lengthways. Re-roll the loin, tie securely and place, seam-side-down, in the prepared tin. Roast for 20 minutes. Reduce the heat to moderate 180°C (350°F/Gas 4), baste the pork with some maple syrup and roast for a further 30 minutes.

Toss together the parsnip, carrots and oil in a large bowl and season if necessary. Add to the roasting tin and roast for a further 30–35 minutes, or until the vegetables are golden and tender. In the last 10 minutes of cooking, baste the pork again with the syrup. Remove the roast pork from the tin, cover with foil and allow to rest for 10 minutes before slicing. Serve with the vegetables and any pan juices.

Serves 4

Blue eye cutlets in a spicy tomato sauce

4 blue eye cutlets, 2.5 cm thick
(about 250 g each)
1¼ cups (250 g) long-grain rice
2 tablespoons oil
1 teaspoon coriander seeds,
lightly crushed
1 teaspoon black mustard seeds
1½ tablespoons sambal oelek
400 g can diced tomatoes
1 teaspoon garam masala
300 g baby English spinach leaves

Preheat the oven to moderate 180°C (350°F/Gas 4). Pat the cutlets dry with paper towels. Bring a large saucepan of water to the boil. Add the rice and cook for 12 minutes, stirring occasionally. Drain well.

Meanwhile, heat 1 tablespoon of the oil in a saucepan over medium heat. When hot, add the coriander and mustard seeds—the mustard seeds should start to pop after 30 seconds. Add the sambal oelek and cook for 30 seconds, then stir in the tomatoes and the garam masala. Bring to the boil, then reduce the.heat to low and simmer, covered, for 6–8 minutes, or until the sauce thickens.

Heat the remaining oil in a large non-stick frying pan over medium heat. Add the cutlets and cook for 1 minute each side, or until evenly browned but not cooked through. Transfer to a 28 cm x 18.5 cm ceramic baking dish. Spoon the tomato sauce over the cutlets and bake for 10 minutes, or until the fish is cooked through.

Meanwhile, wash the spinach and put in a saucepan with just the water clinging to the leaves. Cook, covered, for 1 minute, or until wilted. Serve the fish cutlets topped with sauce, with the spinach and the rice.

Serves 4

Herbed garlic mushrooms with goat's cheese bruschetta

80 g butter
4 cloves garlic, crushed
2/3 cup (20 g) chopped fresh
   flat-leaf parsley
4 large field mushrooms (100 g each),
   stalks removed
4 large slices crusty Italian bread,
   sliced on the diagonal
2 tablespoons olive oil
150 g goat's cheese, at room
   temperature
40 g baby rocket leaves

Preheat the oven to moderate 180°C (350°F/Gas 4). Melt the butter in a small saucepan, add the garlic and parsley, and cook, stirring, for 1 minute, or until well combined. Spoon the mixture evenly over the underside of the mushrooms. Line a baking tray with baking paper. Place the mushrooms on the tray, filling-side-up, and cover with foil. Bake for 20 minutes, or until softened and cooked through.

Towards the end of the mushrooms' cooking time, brush both sides of the bread with the olive oil and grill or chargrill until crisp and golden on both sides.

Spread the bruschetta with the soft goat's cheese and top with the rocket. Cut the hot garlic mushrooms in half and place two halves on each bruschetta, then drizzle with the cooking juices and season with ground black pepper. Serve immediately to prevent the bread from going soggy.

Serves 4

Roasted lamb shanks in rich tomato sauce on polenta

2 tablespoons olive oil
1 large red onion, sliced
4 French-trimmed lamb shanks
  (about 250 g each)
2 cloves garlic, crushed
400 g can chopped tomatoes
½ cup (125 ml) red wine
2 teaspoons chopped fresh rosemary
1 cup (150 g) instant polenta
50 g butter
½ cup (50 g) grated Parmesan

Preheat the oven to warm 160°C (315°F/Gas 2–3). Heat the oil in a 4 litre flameproof casserole dish over medium heat and sauté the onion for 3–4 minutes, or until softening and becoming transparent. Add the lamb shanks and cook for 2–3 minutes, or until lightly browned. Add the garlic, tomato and wine, then bring to the boil and cook for 3–4 minutes. Stir in the rosemary. Season with ¼ teaspoon each of salt and pepper.

Cover and bake for 2 hours. Uncover, return to the oven and simmer for another 15 minutes, or until the lamb just starts to fall off the bone. Check periodically that the sauce is not too dry, adding water if needed.

About 20 minutes before serving, bring 1 litre water to the boil in a saucepan. Add the polenta in a thin stream, whisking continuously, then reduce the heat to very low. Simmer for 8–10 minutes, or until thick and coming away from the side of the saucepan. Stir in the butter and Parmesan. To serve, spoon the polenta onto serving plates, top with the shanks and a little sauce from the casserole over the shanks.

Serves 4

Note: Although this dish has a long cooking time, the preparation is fast.

Baked Mediterranean
pork cutlets

4 large pork loin cutlets, trimmed
2 tablespoons olive oil
2 cloves garlic, finely chopped
1 tablespoon finely chopped fresh
 rosemary
2 tablespoons fresh thyme
2 tablespoons balsamic vinegar
4 Roma tomatoes, halved lengthways
1 large red capsicum (pepper), cut
 into 2 cm slices
4 small zucchini (courgettes), trimmed
 and halved lengthways

Preheat the oven to hot 220°C (425°F/Gas 7) and lightly grease a baking tin. Arrange the pork cutlets in a single layer in the tin. Combine the olive oil, garlic, rosemary, thyme and 1 tablespoon of the balsamic vinegar, then spoon half the mixture over the pork cutlets. Season to taste with salt and black pepper. Cover with plastic wrap and marinate for 20 minutes.

Place 2 tomato halves, cut-side-down, on each pork cutlet and sprinkle the tomatoes with the remaining balsamic vinegar.

Toss the capsicum and zucchini with the remaining herb mixture, then add to the dish around the cutlets. Bake for 45 minutes, or until cooked through and well browned. Season, to taste. Serve the cutlets with the roast vegetables, a green salad and crusty bread.

Serves 4

317

Baked potato with avocado, tomato and corn salsa

4 large potatoes
2 vine-ripened tomatoes, seeded
 and chopped
125 g can corn kernels, drained
2 spring onions, chopped
1 tablespoon lime juice
½ teaspoon sugar
1 avocado, diced
¼ cup (15 g) chopped fresh coriander
 leaves
1 tablespoon sour cream, optional

Preheat the oven to hot 210°C (415°F/ Gas 6–7). Pierce the potatoes all over with a fork. Bake directly on the oven rack for 1 hour, or until tender when tested with a skewer. Leave for about 2 minutes. Cut a cross in the top of each potato and squeeze gently from the base to open (if the potato is still too hot, hold the potato in a clean tea towel).

While the potatoes are cooking, put the tomatoes, corn kernels, spring onions, lime juice and sugar in a bowl and mix well. Add the avocado and coriander leaves. Season. Spoon some mixture onto each potato and, if desired, dollop with the sour cream.

Serves 4

Note: These potatoes can be prepared for cooking very quickly. You can also do a chicken topping. Cook 2 chicken breasts in 2 cups (500 ml) boiling chicken stock for 5 minutes. Remove from the heat and cool in the liquid. Shred the meat. Add 2 tablespoons mayonnaise, 1 teaspoon grated lemon rind and 1 tablespoon baby capers. Toss 3 cups (135 g) shredded rocket with 1 tablespoon extra virgin olive oil, 1 tablespoon balsamic vinegar and 1 sliced avocado. Place some in each potato and top with the chicken mixture. Season to taste.

Tortilla pie

1 tablespoon oil
500 g lean beef mince
35 g packet taco seasoning mix
420 g can Mexican chilli beans, drained
8 flour tortillas
2 cups (250 g) grated Cheddar
300 g Mexican tomato salsa
150 g sour cream
1 avocado, diced

Preheat the oven to moderate 180°C (350°F/Gas 4). Grease a 23 cm pie dish. Heat the oil in a large non-stick frying pan. Add the mince and cook for 5 minutes, or until brown, breaking up the lumps with the back of a spoon. Drain off the excess oil. Add the seasoning mix and cook for 5 minutes. Stir in the beans until heated through.

Lay a tortilla in the base of the pie dish, then spread ½ cup (125 g) of the mince mixture on top. Sprinkle with ¼ cup (30 g) cheese and 1 tablespoon salsa. Continue layering with the remaining tortillas, mince mixture, cheese and salsa, ending with a tortilla sprinkled with a little cheese—it should end up looking like a dome shape.

Bake for 15 minutes, or until all the cheese has melted and browned. Cool slightly, cut into wedges and top with a dollop of sour cream and the diced avocado. Serve with a tomato salad, if desired.

Serves 4

Ham and cheese pasta bake

1½ tablespoons olive oil
1 onion, finely chopped
300 g leg ham, sliced 3 mm thick
and cut into 5 cm lengths
600 ml cream
300 g cooked fresh peas or frozen
peas, thawed
375 g conchiglione (pasta shells)
3 tablespoons roughly chopped
fresh basil
2 cups (250 g) grated mature
Cheddar

Preheat the oven to moderately hot 200°C (400°F/Gas 6) and lightly grease a 2.5 litre ovenproof ceramic dish. Heat 1 tablespoon of the oil in a frying pan over medium heat and cook the onion, stirring frequently for 5 minutes, or until soft. Add the remaining oil, then the ham and cook, stirring, for 1 minute. Pour the cream into the pan, bring to the boil, then reduce the heat and simmer for 6 minutes. Add the peas and cook for another 2–4 minutes, or until the mixture has reduced and thickened slightly. Season with freshly ground black pepper.

Meanwhile, cook the pasta in a large saucepan of rapidly boiling salted water according to the packet instructions until *al dente*. Drain and return to the pan.

Add the cream sauce to the pasta, then the basil and three quarters of the cheese. Stir well and season. Transfer the mixture to the prepared dish, sprinkle on the remaining cheese and bake for 20 minutes, or until the top is golden brown.

Serves 4

Note: Other pasta shapes such as spirals, farfalle, fusilli or macaroni are suitable for this dish.

Thai ginger fish with coriander butter

60 g butter, at room temperature
1 tablespoon finely chopped fresh
   coriander leaves
2 tablespoons lime juice
1 tablespoon oil
1 tablespoon grated palm sugar
4 fresh long red chillies, seeded
   and chopped
2 stems lemon grass, trimmed
4 firm white fish fillets (blue eye
   or John Dory), (about 200 g each)
1 lime, thinly sliced
1 tablespoon finely shredded
   fresh ginger

Thoroughly mix the butter and coriander and roll it into a log. Wrap the log in plastic wrap and chill in the refrigerator until required.

Preheat the oven to moderately hot 200°C (400°F/Gas 6). Combine the lime juice, oil, palm sugar and chilli in a small non-metallic bowl and stir until the sugar has dissolved. Cut the lemon grass into halves.

Place a piece of lemon grass in the centre of a sheet of foil large enough to fully enclose one fillet. Place a fish fillet on top and smear the surface with the lime juice mixture. Top with some lime slices and ginger shreds, then wrap into a secure parcel. Repeat with the remaining ingredients to make four parcels.

Place the parcels in an ovenproof dish and bake for 8–10 minutes, or until the fish flakes easily when tested with a fork.

To serve, place the parcels on individual serving plates and serve open with slices of coriander butter, steamed rice and steamed greens.

Serves 4

Sausage and bean hotpot with roasted orange sweet potato

1 kg spicy Italian-style sausages
2 cloves garlic, roughly chopped
2 x 400 g cans cannellini beans
2 x 425 g cans crushed tomatoes
2 teaspoons Dijon mustard
750 g orange sweet potato, cut
   into 3 cm cubes
2 tablespoons olive oil
2 tablespoons coarsely chopped
   fresh flat-leaf parsley

Preheat the oven to moderately hot 200°C (400°F/Gas 6). Cook the sausages in a large frying pan over medium heat for 5–7 minutes, or until golden. Cut into 5 cm pieces and place in a 4 litre casserole dish. Add the garlic, beans, tomato, mustard and 2 tablespoons water to the dish and season with pepper. Stir well and cover with a lid. Place in the oven.

Meanwhile, toss the sweet potato with the oil and place snugly in a baking dish. Sprinkle with salt. Place in the oven with the casserole dish and bake for 25 minutes. Uncover the casserole dish and bake for another 10–15 minutes, or until the hotpot is golden and bubbling and the sweet potato is soft and lightly golden brown. Serve the hotpot garnished with the parsley and the sweet potato on the side.

Serves 4

Vegetable bake

400 g potatoes, thinly sliced lengthways
60 g butter, melted
1½–2 teaspoons finely chopped fresh thyme
400 g pumpkin, thinly sliced
300 g zucchini (courgettes), thinly sliced lengthways
1 cup (250 ml) tomato pasta sauce
½ cup (50 g) grated Parmesan

Preheat the oven to warm 170°C (325°F/Gas 3). Grease a 1.5 litre rectangular ovenproof dish. Combine the potato with one third each of the butter and thyme. Season, then place in the base of the prepared dish.

Combine the pumpkin and another third of the butter and thyme. Season and press onto the potato. Combine the zucchini with the remaining butter and thyme. Season and press onto the pumpkin.

Spread the pasta sauce evenly over the top and cover with greased foil. Bake for 45 minutes, remove the foil and sprinkle with the grated Parmesan. Bake for another 15 minutes, or until the top is golden brown and the vegetables are cooked through. Can be served with a salad and crusty bread, if desired.

Serves 4

Chicken and leek pies

60 g butter
1 leek, thinly sliced
4 chicken breasts (about 200 g each)
50 g plain flour
1 cup (250 ml) chicken and herb
stock
300 ml cream
1 cup (155 g) fresh or frozen peas,
blanched
1 sheet ready-rolled puff pastry,
thawed

Melt the butter in a saucepan over medium heat and cook the leek for 2–3 minutes, or until soft. Add the chicken and cook for 45 minutes, or until cooked. Add the flour and cook, stirring, until it starts to bubble. Add the stock and cook until the mixture starts to thicken. Add the cream, reserving 1 tablespoon to glaze the pastry. Cook until the mixture just starts to boil. Stir in the peas. Season. Remove from the heat. Preheat the oven to moderately hot 200°C (400°F/Gas 6).

Divide the filling among four individual pie dishes or ramekins. Top with a circle of pastry, cut just bigger than the top of the dish, then press around the edges to seal. Brush the surface with the reserved cream. Make a small slit in the top to allow steam to escape. Place the dishes on a metal tray and bake for 20–25 minutes, or until the pastry is golden. Serve with a green salad.

Serves 4

Sweet

Strawberries with balsamic vinegar

750 g ripe small strawberries
¼ cup (60 g) caster sugar
2 tablespoons balsamic vinegar
½ cup (125 g) mascarpone

Wipe the strawberries with a clean damp cloth and carefully remove the green stalks. If the strawberries are large, cut each one in half.

Place all the strawberries in a large glass bowl, sprinkle the caster sugar evenly over the top and toss gently to coat. Set aside for 2 hours to macerate, then sprinkle the balsamic vinegar over the strawberries. Toss them again, then refrigerate for about 30 minutes.

Spoon the strawberries into four glasses, drizzle with the syrup and top with a dollop of mascarpone.

Serves 4

Note: If you leave the strawberries for more than 2 hours, it is best to refrigerate them.

Panna cotta with passionfruit sauce

light olive oil, for brushing
2½ teaspoons powdered gelatine
300 ml goat's milk or normal milk
300 ml cream
2 tablespoons caster sugar
1 teaspoon vanilla essence

Passionfruit sauce
3 tablespoons sugar
⅓ cup (90 g) fresh passionfruit pulp

Lightly brush four 150 ml moulds or ramekins with light olive oil. Place the gelatine and 2 tablespoons water in a small bowl. Place over a bowl of hot water and stir until dissolved.

Put the milk, cream and caster sugar in a small saucepan. Gently heat to just under boiling point, stirring so all the sugar dissolves. Remove from the heat and whisk in the gelatine mixture until dissolved. Leave to cool for a few minutes then stir in the vanilla essence. Pour into the moulds and refrigerate for 6 hours, or until set.

Meanwhile, to make the passionfruit sauce, place the sugar and ½ cup (125 ml) water in a small saucepan over medium heat and stir for 3 minutes, or until the sugar has dissolved. Remove from the heat and stir in the passionfruit pulp. Pour into a small jug and refrigerate until required. Lightly run a knife around the side of each mould and unmould onto serving plates. Spoon the passionfruit sauce over the top and serve chilled.

Serves 4

Note: Although these require 6 hours refrigeration, they are quick to prepare.

Flourless chocolate cake

½ cup (95 g) soft brown sugar
6 eggs
400 g dark chocolate
1 tablespoon Grand Marnier
1 teaspoon ground cinnamon
300 ml double thick cream,
    plus extra, to serve
icing sugar, to dust
strawberries, to serve

Preheat the oven to moderate 180°C (350°F/Gas 4). Grease a 23 cm round cake tin and line the base with baking paper. Beat the sugar and eggs in a bowl for 10 minutes, or until creamy.

Meanwhile, chop the chocolate into small even-size pieces and place in a heatproof bowl. Bring a saucepan of water to the boil, then remove from the heat. Sit the bowl over the pan, making sure the base of the bowl does not touch the water. Stir occasionally until the chocolate has melted. Place the Grand Marnier, cinnamon, egg mixture and melted chocolate in a bowl and mix together. Stir the cream very gently by hand 2–3 times and then fold into the chocolate mixture.

Pour the mixture into the prepared tin and bake for 1 hour, or until a skewer comes out clean. Allow to cool in the tin, then turn out onto a cake rack when cold. Cut into slices, dust with icing sugar and serve with a dollop of cream and strawberries.

Serves 8

Note: This is a moist cake and will sink a little in the middle. If you prefer, use brandy, Tia Maria or Cointreau instead of Grand Marnier.

Coconut lime ice cream

¼ cup (25 g) desiccated coconut
1½ tablespoons grated lime rind
⅓ cup (80 ml) lime juice
4 tablespoons coconut milk powder
1 litre good-quality vanilla ice cream,
  softened
coconut macaroon biscuits, to serve

Combine the desiccated coconut, grated lime rind, lime juice and coconut milk powder in a bowl and mix well.

Add the coconut mixture to the ice cream and fold through with a large metal spoon until evenly incorporated. Work quickly so that the ice cream does not melt. Return the mixture to the freezer and freeze for 30 minutes to firm. To serve, place 3 scoops in four latté glasses and serve with some coconut macaroon biscuits on the side.

Serves 4

Apple galettes

¼ cup (90 g) honey
pinch of mixed spice
2 large green apples (375 g)
2 sheets ready-rolled puff pastry
3 tablespoons ground almonds
2 teaspoons icing sugar
40 g butter, cubed
thick cream, to serve

Preheat the oven to hot 210°C (415°F/Gas 6–7). Place the honey, mixed spice and ⅔ cup (170 ml) water in a saucepan, and stir to combine. Peel, core and thinly slice the apples. Add to the pan, cover and cook over low heat for 8 minutes, or until the apple is tender. Stir gently halfway through cooking. Cool and drain the apple, reserving the juice. Return the juice to the pan and boil for 10 minutes, or until syrupy.

Cut the puff pastry into four 12 cm rounds, place on a lightly greased baking tray and sprinkle with the ground almonds. Arrange the apple slices over the pastry in a spiral pattern. Dust heavily with the icing sugar and dot the butter over the apples. Bake for 15–20 minutes, or until puffed and golden. Drizzle with the syrup and serve with cream.

Serves 4

Pineapple gratin

800 g ripe pineapple, cut into
  1.5 cm cubes
¼ cup (60 ml) dark rum
2 tablespoons unsalted butter
1 teaspoon vanilla essence
¼ cup (45 g) soft brown sugar
½ teaspoon ground ginger
300 g sour cream
¼ cup (60 ml) cream
1 teaspoon finely grated lemon rind
½ cup (95 g) soft brown sugar,
  to sprinkle, extra

Place the pineapple, rum, butter, vanilla, sugar and ginger in a large saucepan and cook, stirring occasionally, for 8–10 minutes, or until caramelised. Remove from the heat.

Divide the pineapple among four individual gratin dishes and allow it to cool slightly.

Combine the sour cream, cream and lemon rind in a bowl, then spoon evenly over the pineapple. Sprinkle the extra sugar over each gratin.

Cook the gratins under a hot grill for 4–5 minutes, or until the sugar has melted and caramelised. Take care not to burn them. Serve immediately.

Serves 4

Poached pears in saffron citrus syrup

1 vanilla bean
½ teaspoon firmly packed saffron
  threads
¾ cup (185 g) caster sugar
2 teaspoons grated lemon rind
4 pears, peeled, stalks intact
whipped cream, to serve, optional
biscotti, to serve, optional

Place the vanilla bean, saffron threads, caster sugar and lemon rind in a saucepan with 1 litre water, and mix well. Stir over low heat until the sugar dissolves. Bring to the boil, then reduce the heat and simmer for 10–12 minutes, or until slightly reduced and syrupy.

Add the pears and cook, covered, for 12–15 minutes, or until tender when tested with a metal skewer. Turn the pears over with a slotted spoon halfway through cooking. Once cooked, remove from the syrup.

Bring to the boil, and cook for 10 minutes, or until the syrup has halved and thickened slightly. Remove the vanilla bean and serve the syrup drizzled over the pears with whipped cream and biscotti.

Serves 4

Tiramisu cake

510 g packet French vanilla
  cake mix
3 eggs
⅓ cup (80 ml) vegetable oil
300 ml thick cream
¼ cup (30 g) icing sugar
250 g mascarpone, chilled
100 ml Kahlua
1½ tablespoons instant coffee

Preheat the oven to moderate 180°C (350°F/Gas 4). Grease a 22 cm square cake tin and line the base with baking paper. Beat the cake mix, eggs, oil and 290 ml water in a large bowl with electric beaters on low speed for 30 seconds. Increase the speed and beat for 2 minutes, or until well combined. Pour into the tin and bake for 35–40 minutes, or until a skewer comes out clean when inserted into the centre of the cake. Turn out onto a wire rack to cool. Beat the cream and sugar with a whisk until stiff. Fold in the mascarpone and 2 teaspoons of the Kahlua. Combine the coffee and the remaining Kahlua, stirring until the coffee has dissolved.

Cut the cake in half horizontally. Place the base of the cake on a serving plate and brush liberally with the coffee mixture, then spread one third of the cream mixture on top. Top with the other layer of cake and brush with the remaining coffee mixture. Spread the remaining cream mixture over the top and sides. If desired, sprinkle the surface with grated chocolate to serve.

Serves 6–8

Grilled figs with amaretto mascarpone

¼ cup (60 g) caster sugar
¼ cup (60 ml) cream
½ teaspoon vanilla essence
½ cup (110 g) mascarpone
50 ml amaretto
1½ tablespoons caster sugar, extra
¼ cup (35 g) blanched almonds, finely chopped
½ teaspoon ground cinnamon
6 fresh figs, halved

Line a baking tray with foil. Place the caster sugar and ¼ cup (60 ml) water in a small saucepan and stir over low heat until the sugar has dissolved, brushing down the side of the pan with a clean brush dipped in water if any crystals appear. Bring to the boil and cook, without stirring, for about 8 minutes, swirling occasionally until the mixture is golden. Quickly remove the pan from the heat and carefully pour in the cream, stirring constantly until smooth, then stir in the vanilla.

To make the amaretto mascarpone, place the mascarpone, amaretto and 2 teaspoons of the extra caster sugar in a bowl and mix together well.

Combine the chopped almonds, cinnamon and remaining caster sugar on a plate.

Press the cut side of each fig half into the almond mixture, then place, cut-side-up, onto the baking tray. Cook under a hot grill for 4–5 minutes, or until the sugar has caramelised and the almonds are nicely toasted — watch carefully to prevent burning.

Arrange three fig halves on each plate, place a dollop of the amaretto mascarpone to the side and drizzle with the sauce.

Serves 4

Baby coffee and walnut sour cream cakes

3/4 cup (75 g) walnuts
2/3 cup (155 g) firmly packed soft
 brown sugar
125 g unsalted butter, softened
2 eggs, lightly beaten
1 cup (125 g) self-raising flour
1/3 cup (80 g) sour cream
1 tablespoon coffee and
 chicory essence

Preheat the oven to warm 160°C (315°F/Gas 2–3). Lightly grease two 12-hole 1/4 cup (60 ml) baby muffin tins. Process the walnuts and 1/4 cup (45 g) of the brown sugar in a food processor until the walnuts are roughly chopped into small pieces. Transfer to a bowl.

Cream the butter and remaining sugar together in the food processor until pale and creamy. With the motor running, gradually add the egg and process until smooth. Add the flour and blend until well mixed. Add the sour cream and essence and process until thoroughly mixed.

Spoon half a teaspoon of the walnut and sugar mixture into the base of each muffin hole, followed by a teaspoon of the cake mixture. Sprinkle a little more walnut mixture over the top, a little more cake mixture and top with the remaining walnut mixture. Bake for 20 minutes, or until risen and springy to the touch. Leave in the tins for 5 minutes. Remove the cakes using the handle of a teaspoon to loosen the side and base, then transfer to a wire rack to cool completely.

Makes 24

Individual self-saucing chocolate puddings

¾ cup (90 g) self-raising flour
1 tablespoon cocoa powder, plus
  3 teaspoons cocoa powder, extra
½ cup (125 g) caster sugar
1 egg, lightly beaten
¼ cup (60 ml) milk
60 g butter, melted
⅓ cup (60 g) soft brown sugar
icing sugar, to dust

Preheat the oven to moderate 180°C (350°F/Gas 4). Lightly grease four ½ cup (125 ml) ovenproof dishes. Sift the flour and 1 tablespoon cocoa into a small bowl and add the sugar. Stir in the combined egg, milk and butter, and mix together well.

Spoon the mixture into the dishes and sprinkle with the combined sugar and extra cocoa powder. Place on a baking tray and carefully pour ¼ cup (60 ml) boiling water, over the back of a metal spoon for even coverage, over each pudding. Bake the puddings for 15–20 minutes, or until a skewer comes out clean when inserted halfway in. Dust with icing sugar, then serve immediately with cream or ice cream.

Serves 4

Note: When testing whether the puddings are ready, insert your skewer at an angle. This way there is a larger area being checked.

Passionfruit bavarois

2 x 170 g cans passionfruit in syrup
300 g silken tofu, chopped
600 ml buttermilk
2 tablespoons caster sugar
1 teaspoon vanilla essence
6 teaspoons gelatine
3/4 cup (185 ml) fresh passionfruit pulp
250 g strawberries, halved

Push the passionfruit in syrup through a sieve. Discard the seeds, then place the syrup, tofu, buttermilk, sugar and vanilla in a blender and blend for 90 seconds on high to mix thoroughly. Leave in the blender.

Place 1/3 cup (80 ml) water in a heatproof bowl and sprinkle the gelatine on top. Stand the bowl in a saucepan of very hot water and stir until the gelatine has dissolved and the mixture is smooth. Cool slightly.

Place eight 200 ml dariole moulds in a baking dish. Add the gelatine mixture to the blender and mix on high for 1 minute. Pour into the dariole moulds, cover the dish with plastic wrap and chill overnight.

When ready to serve, carefully run a spatula around the edge of each mould and dip the bases into very hot water for 2 seconds. Turn each out onto a plate and spoon the passionfruit pulp around the bases. Garnish with the halved strawberries and serve.

Serves 8

Note: Plan ahead with these as they need to be refrigerated overnight. They are very quick to prepare.

Bread and butter pudding

50 g unsalted butter
8 thick slices day-old white bread
1 teaspoon ground cinnamon
2 tablespoons sultanas
3 eggs
1 egg yolk
3 tablespoons caster sugar
1 cup (250 ml) milk
2 cups (500 ml) cream
½ teaspoon vanilla essence
1 tablespoon demerara sugar

Preheat the oven to moderate 180°C (350°F/Gas 4). Melt 10 g of the butter and use to brush a 1.5 litre ovenproof dish. Spread the bread very lightly with the remaining butter and cut each slice in half diagonally. Layer the bread in the prepared dish, sprinkling the cinnamon and sultanas between each layer.

Lightly whisk together the eggs, egg yolk and caster sugar in a large bowl. Heat the milk with the cream until just warm and stir in the vanilla. Whisk the cream mixture into the egg mixture. Strain the custard over the layered bread, then leave for 5 minutes before sprinkling with the demerara sugar.

Bake for 30 minutes, or until the custard has set and the bread is golden brown. Serve warm or at room temperature.

Serves 4

Raspberry mousse

300 g fresh or thawed frozen
raspberries
400 g vanilla fromage frais
or whipped yoghurt
1 tablespoon gelatine
2 egg whites
2 tablespoons sugar
raspberries, extra, to garnish

Mash the raspberries roughly with
a fork. Combine in a large bowl with
the fromage frais.

Put 2 tablespoons hot water in a
small heatproof bowl and sprinkle
with the gelatine. Stand the bowl in
a saucepan of very hot water, and
stir until the gelatine has dissolved
and the mixture is smooth. Cool
slightly, then whisk through the
raspberry mixture.

Using electric beaters, beat the egg
whites in a clean, dry bowl until soft
peaks form, then add the sugar,
1 tablespoon at a time, beating until
dissolved. Gently fold through the
berry mixture. Spoon into eight
150 ml moulds, and refrigerate for
2 hours, or until set. Turn out onto
a serving plate and serve with the
extra raspberries.

Serves 8

Note: Allow 2 hours for refrigeration
for this dessert. The actual preparing
of it doesn't take long at all.

Peaches poached in wine

4 just-ripe yellow-fleshed freestone
  peaches
2 cups (500 ml) sweet white wine
  such as Sauternes
¼ cup (60 ml) orange liqueur
1 cinnamon stick
1 cup (250 g) sugar
1 vanilla bean, split
8 fresh mint leaves
mascarpone or crème fraîche,
  to serve

Cut a small cross in the base of each peach. Immerse the peaches in boiling water for 30 seconds, then drain and cool slightly. Peel off the skin, cut in half and carefully remove the stones.

Place the wine, liqueur, cinnamon stick, sugar and vanilla bean in a deep frying pan large enough to hold the peach halves in a single layer. Heat, stirring, until the sugar dissolves. Bring to the boil, then reduce the heat and simmer for 5 minutes. Add the peaches and simmer for 4 minutes, turning them halfway. Remove with a slotted spoon. Simmer the syrup for 6–8 minutes, or until thick. Strain.

Arrange the peaches on a serving platter, cut-side-up. Spoon the syrup over the top and garnish each half with a mint leaf. Serve the peaches warm or chilled, with a dollop of mascarpone or crème fraîche.

Serves 4

Note: There are two types of peach, freestone and clingstone. As the names imply, clingstone indicates that the flesh will cling to the stone whereas the stones in freestone peaches are easily removed without breaking up the flesh. Each has a variety with either yellow or white flesh, and all these peaches are equally delicious.

Mango ice cream in brandy snap baskets

400 g frozen mango
½ cup (125 g) caster sugar
¼ cup (60 ml) mango or apricot
 nectar
300 ml cream
6 ready-made brandy snap baskets
mango slices, to garnish
fresh mint sprigs, to garnish

Defrost the mango until it is soft enough to mash but still icy. Place in a large bowl, and add the sugar and mango nectar. Stir for 1–2 minutes, or until the sugar has dissolved.

Beat the cream in a bowl until stiff peaks form. Gently fold the cream into the mango mixture. Spoon the mixture into a deep tray or plastic container, cover and freeze for 1 hour 30 minutes, or until half-frozen. Quickly spoon the mixture into a food processor. Process for 30 seconds, or until smooth. Return to the tray, cover and freeze completely. Remove the ice cream from the freezer 10 minutes before serving, to allow it to soften a little. To serve, place 2 scoops ice cream in each brandy snap basket, and garnish with the mango slices and sprigs of mint.

Serves 6

Note: You have to allow for freezing time for this ice cream but preparing it for freezing doesn't take very long. The ice cream should be frozen for at least 8 hours before serving and can be kept frozen for up to three weeks. When available, use fresh mangoes. Purée the flesh of 3–4 large mangoes in a food processor.

Chocolate croissant pudding

4 croissants, torn into pieces
100 g dark chocolate, chopped
    into pieces
4 eggs
⅓ cup (90 g) caster sugar
1 cup (250 ml) milk
1 cup (250 ml) cream
½ teaspoon grated orange rind
⅓ cup (80 ml) orange juice
2 tablespoons coarsely chopped
    hazelnuts

Preheat the oven to moderate 180°C (350°F/Gas 4). Grease the base and side of a 20 cm deep-sided cake tin and line the bottom of the tin with baking paper.

Place the croissant pieces in the tin, then scatter evenly with chocolate.

Beat the eggs and sugar together until pale and creamy.

Heat the milk and cream in a saucepan to almost boiling, then remove from the heat. Gradually pour into the egg mixture, stirring constantly. Add the orange rind and juice and stir well.

Slowly pour the mixture over the croissants, allowing the liquid to be absorbed before adding more. Sprinkle the top with the hazelnuts and bake for 45 minutes, or until a skewer comes out clean when inserted in the centre.

Cool for 10 minutes. Run a knife around the edge, then turn out and invert. Cut into wedges and serve warm with cream, if desired.

Serves 6–8

Coconut, ginger and lime cake

150 g unsalted butter, softened
3/4 cup (185 g) caster sugar
2 teaspoons grated lime rind
2 eggs, lightly beaten
1/4 cup (55 g) finely chopped glacé ginger
1 3/4 cups (215 g) self-raising flour
1/2 cup (45 g) desiccated coconut
3/4 cup (185 ml) milk

Preheat the oven to moderate 180°C (350°F/Gas 4). Grease a 22 x 12 cm loaf tin and line the base with baking paper. Beat the butter, sugar and lime rind in a bowl with electric beaters until pale and creamy.

Add the egg gradually, beating well between each addition, then add the ginger. Fold in the sifted flour and the coconut alternately with the milk. Spoon the mixture into the prepared tin and smooth the surface. Bake for 50 minutes, or until a skewer comes out clean when inserted into the centre of the cake. Leave in the tin for 5 minutes then turn onto a wire rack to cool. If desired, garnish with lime slices and lime zest and serve with ice cream.

Serves 8–10

Note: Prepare this delicious cake in a short time, then forget about it while it bakes to perfection.

Summer fruit compote

2 cups (500 g) caster sugar
3 cups (750 ml) white wine, such
  as Chardonnay
2 teaspoons finely grated lime rind
¼ cup (60 ml) lime juice
2 mangoes
3 freestone peaches
3 nectarines
vanilla ice cream, to serve

Place the sugar, white wine, lime rind and juice in a large saucepan. Stir over low heat for 3 minutes, or until the sugar has dissolved. Bring to the boil, then reduce the heat and simmer for 2 minutes. Keep warm.

Cut the cheeks from the mangoes, then remove the skin. Cut each mango cheek into 6 thick wedges. Place the mango in a large serving bowl. Cut a cross in one end of the peaches and nectarines, and plunge them into a bowl of boiling water, and then into cold water. Peel and cut into 4 wedges each, discarding the stones. Add to the mango.

Pour the warm syrup over the fruit, and refrigerate, covered, for 2–3 hours. To serve, return to room temperature and serve with ice cream.

Serves 6

Note: You can leave the peaches and nectarines unpeeled, if preferred. Don't forget to allow for the refrigeration time.

Strawberry ice cream with strawberry sauce

500 g strawberries, hulled, washed
and sliced
2 tablespoons caster sugar
2 tablespoons Cointreau or fresh
orange juice
500 ml good-quality vanilla ice cream,
slightly softened
125 g blueberries, optional

Place the strawberries in a small
saucepan, add the sugar and
Cointreau and cook over low heat for
5 minutes, or until softened and the
juices are released. Remove from the
heat and refrigerate.

Place half the strawberry mixture in
a food processor or blender and
process for 20–30 seconds, or until
smooth. Spoon the ice cream into
the food processor and process for
10 seconds, or until well combined
with the strawberry mixture. Pour into
a rectangular tin and return to the
freezer for 2–3 hours, or until firm.
Serve the ice cream with the reserved
strawberry sauce and blueberries.

Serves 4

Note: This ice cream is ready for the
freezer in a very short time. You can
freeze it overnight if you prefer.

Plum crumble cake

¾ cup (165 g) demerara sugar
2 cups (250 g) self-raising flour
150 g unsalted butter
1 egg
825 g can plums in syrup, drained
   and thinly sliced
1½ teaspoons ground cinnamon
⅔ cup (100 g) blanched almonds,
   chopped

Preheat the oven to moderate 180°C (350°F/Gas 4). Grease a 20 cm shallow sandwich tin and line the base with baking paper. Blend the sugar, flour and butter in a food processor in short bursts until the mixture is combined and crumbly.

Add the egg and process until well combined. Press half the mixture onto the base of the tin. Arrange the plum slices evenly over the dough, then sprinkle with the cinnamon.

Knead the almonds lightly into the remaining dough, then press onto the plum layer. Bake for 50 minutes, or until a skewer comes out clean when inserted into the centre of the cake. Leave in the tin for 15 minutes before carefully turning out onto a wire rack to cool slightly. Delicious served warm with thick cream.

Serves 8

Note: Although you have to leave time for this to cool after baking, the preparation time is very quick.

Winter fruit in orange ginger syrup

¼ cup (60 g) caster sugar
¼ cup (60 ml) orange juice
2 strips orange rind
1 cinnamon stick
250 g dried fruit salad, large
   pieces cut in half
100 g pitted dried dates
1 teaspoon grated fresh ginger
200 g low-fat plain yoghurt

Place the caster sugar, orange juice, orange rind, cinnamon stick and 1½ cups (375 ml) water in a large saucepan. Stir over low heat until the caster sugar dissolves, then increase the heat and simmer, without stirring, for 5 minutes, or until the syrup mixture has thickened slightly.

Add the dried fruit salad, dates and ginger, and toss well. Cover and simmer over low heat for 5 minutes, or until the fruit has softened. Remove from the heat and set aside, covered, for 5 minutes. Discard the orange rind and cinnamon stick. If serving cold, remove from the saucepan and allow to cool.

Place the fruits in individual serving dishes, top with the yoghurt and drizzle a little of the syrup over the top. Serve immediately.

Serves 4

Mini passionfruit almond cakes with lime curd

⅓ cup (60 g) ground almonds
2 tablespoons plain flour, sifted
100 g icing sugar, plus extra to dust
1 teaspoon finely grated lime rind
pulp from 1 passionfruit
120 g unsalted butter, melted
2 eggs
2 tablespoons lime juice

Preheat the oven to warm 170°C (325°F/Gas 3). Lightly grease eight 30 ml patty tins. Place the ground almonds, flour, 60 g icing sugar, lime rind, passionfruit pulp and half the butter in a bowl. Separate the eggs, reserve 1 egg yolk and discard the other. Place the egg whites in a clean, dry bowl and beat to soft peaks. Gently fold into the almond mixture. Spoon into the prepared patty tins and bake for 10–15 minutes, or until the cakes are puffed and golden.

Meanwhile, place the lime juice, remaining butter and sifted remaining icing sugar in a small saucepan, and heat to a simmer, stirring until all the sugar has dissolved. Remove from the heat and cool slightly, then whisk in the reserved egg yolk. Return to very low heat and stir for 5 minutes, or until thickened. Do not boil.

Leave the cakes to stand in the tins for 5 minutes before gently removing. Serve two cakes per person, dusted with extra icing sugar and drizzled with a little lime curd. Serve with cream or ice cream, if desired.

Serves 4

Note: Alternatively, the lime curd can be cooled and spread over the tops of the cakes.

Crème caramel

canola oil spray
⅓ cup (90 g) caster sugar
1½ cups (375 ml) skim milk
2 eggs
1½ tablespoons caster sugar, extra
½ teaspoon vanilla essence
1 teaspoon maple syrup

Preheat the oven to warm 160°C (315°F/Gas 2–3). Lightly spray four ½ cup (125 ml) ovenproof ramekins (7.5 cm diameter) with canola oil. Put the caster sugar and 1½ tablespoons water in a small heavy-based saucepan. Stir over low heat until the sugar is dissolved. Bring to the boil, then reduce the heat and simmer until the syrup turns straw-coloured and begins to caramelise. Remove from the heat and divide among the ramekins, coating the bases evenly.

Heat the milk in a small saucepan with a pinch of salt over low heat until almost boiling. Put the eggs and extra sugar in a bowl and whisk together for 2 minutes. Stir in the warm milk, vanilla and maple syrup. Strain into a jug and divide among the ramekins.

Place the ramekins in a baking dish and add enough boiling water to reach halfway up the sides of the ramekins. Bake for 35 minutes, or until the custards are set. Remove from the dish and leave to cool completely. Refrigerate for 2 hours, or until chilled. To serve, carefully run a knife around the edge of each custard. Invert the ramekins onto plates and lift off, giving them a gentle shake.

Serves 4

Note: These can be served warm.

Lemon frozen yoghurt

1 litre low-fat vanilla yoghurt
3/4 cup (185 ml) lemon juice
3/4 cup (185 g) caster sugar
1/4 cup (60 ml) light corn syrup
1 teaspoon finely grated lemon rind
1/2 teaspoon vanilla essence

Place the yoghurt in a fine sieve over a bowl and leave to drain in the refrigerator for at least 2 hours. Discard the liquid that drains off.

Place the remaining ingredients in a bowl and whisk together until the sugar dissolves. Add the drained yoghurt and whisk in well.

If you have an ice-cream machine, pour the mixture into it and churn according to the maker's instructions. Otherwise, place the mixture in a shallow metal tray and freeze for 2 hours, or until the mixture is frozen around the edges. Transfer to a large bowl and beat until smooth. Repeat this step three times. For the final freezing, place in an airtight container, cover the surface with a piece of greaseproof paper and a lid, and freeze for 4 hours or overnight. Serve in parfait glasses.

Serves 6–8

Sand cake

185 g unsalted butter, softened
2 teaspoons vanilla essence
1 cup (250 g) caster sugar
3 eggs
1½ cups (185 g) self-raising flour
⅓ cup (60 g) rice flour
⅓ cup (80 ml) milk

Preheat the oven to moderate 180°C (350°F/Gas 4). Grease a 23 cm square tin and line the base with baking paper.

Beat the butter, vanilla, sugar, eggs, flours and milk with electric beaters until combined, then beat at medium speed for 3 minutes, or until thick and creamy.

Pour the mixture into the prepared tin and smooth the surface. Bake for 50 minutes, or until a skewer comes out clean when inserted into the centre of the cake. Leave for 10 minutes in the tin then turn out onto a wire rack to cool.

Serves 8–10

Individual sticky date cakes

1½ cups (270 g) pitted dates,
chopped
1 teaspoon bicarbonate of soda
150 g unsalted butter, chopped
1½ cups (185 g) self-raising flour
265 g firmly packed soft brown sugar
2 eggs, lightly beaten
2 tablespoons golden syrup
¾ cup (185 ml) cream

Preheat the oven to moderate 180°C (350°F/Gas 4). Grease six 1 cup (250 ml) muffin holes. Place the dates and 1 cup (250 ml) water in a saucepan, bring to the boil, then remove from the heat and stir in the bicarbonate of soda. Add 60 g of the butter and stir until melted. Sift the flour into a large bowl, add ⅔ cup (125 g) of the sugar and stir. Make a well in the centre, add the date mixture and egg and stir until just combined. Spoon evenly into the holes and bake for 20 minutes, or until a skewer comes out clean when inserted into the centre.

To make the sauce, place the golden syrup, cream, the remaining butter and the remaining sugar in a small saucepan and stir over low heat for 3–4 minutes, or until the sugar has dissolved. Bring to the boil, then reduce the heat and simmer, stirring occasionally, for 2 minutes. To serve, turn the cakes onto serving plates, pierce the cakes a few times with a skewer and drizzle with the sauce. Serve with ice cream, if desired.

Makes 6

Dried apricot fool

30 g finely chopped glacé ginger
175 g dried apricots, chopped
2 egg whites
2 tablespoons caster sugar
1 tablespoon shredded coconut,
   toasted

Place the ginger, apricots and ⅓ cup (80 ml) water in a small saucepan. Cook, covered, over very low heat for 5 minutes, stirring occasionally. Remove from the heat and allow to cool completely.

Using electric beaters, beat the egg whites in a clean, dry bowl until soft peaks form. Add the caster sugar and beat for 3 minutes, or until thick and glossy. Quickly and gently fold the cooled apricot mixture into the egg mixture and divide among four chilled serving glasses. Scatter the coconut over the top and serve immediately.

Serves 4

Note: The apricots can scorch easily, so cook over low heat. Serve immediately, or the egg white will slowly break down and lose volume.

No-bake chocolate squares

100 g shortbread biscuits, roughly
  crushed
120 g pistachios, shelled
150 g hazelnuts, toasted and skinned
100 g glacé cherries, roughly
  chopped
300 g good-quality dark (not bitter)
  chocolate
200 g unsalted butter
1 teaspoon instant coffee powder
2 eggs, lightly beaten

Lightly grease an 18 x 27 cm baking tin and line with baking paper, hanging over the two long sides. Combine the biscuits, pistachios, 90 g hazelnuts, and half the cherries.

Chop the chocolate and butter into small even-sized pieces and place in a heatproof bowl. Bring a saucepan of water to the boil and remove from the heat. Sit the bowl over the pan— ensure the bowl doesn't touch the water. Allow to stand, stirring occasionally, until the chocolate and butter have melted. Remove the bowl from the pan and when the mixture has cooled slightly, mix in the coffee and eggs. Pour over the nut mixture and mix well.

Pour the slice mixture into the tin and pat down well. Roughly chop the remaining hazelnuts and sprinkle over the top with the remaining cherries. Refrigerate overnight.

Remove from the tin and trim the edges of the slice before cutting into pieces. Keep in the refrigerator.

Makes 18 pieces

Note: Toast the hazelnuts in a moderate 180°C (350°F/Gas 4) oven for 5–10 minutes, or until light golden. Tip onto a clean tea towel and rub gently to remove the skins.

Lemon granita

1¼ cups (315 ml) lemon juice
1 tablespoon lemon zest
200 g caster sugar

Place the lemon juice, lemon zest and caster sugar in a small saucepan and stir over low heat for 5 minutes, or until the sugar is dissolved. Remove from the heat and leave to cool.

Add 2 cups (500 ml) water to the juice mixture and mix together well. Pour the mixture into a shallow 30 x 20 cm metal container and place in the freezer until the mixture is beginning to freeze around the edges. Scrape the frozen sections back into the mixture with a fork. Repeat every 30 minutes until the mixture has even-size ice crystals. Beat the mixture with a fork just before serving. To serve, spoon the lemon granita into six chilled glasses.

Serves 6

Note: Although granita is easy and quick to prepare, you do have to allow for the freezing time.

Index

INDEX

Photographers: Cris Cordeiro, Craig Cranko, Joe Filshie, Ian Hofstetter,
Tony Lyons, Andre Martin, Rob Reichenfeld, Brett Stevens

Food Stylists: Marie-Hélène Clauzon, Jane Collins, Sarah de Nardi, Georgina Dolling,
Carolyn Fienberg, Mary Harris, Cherise Koch, Michelle Noerianto

Food Preparation: Alison Adams, Justine Johnson, Valli Little, Kate Murdoch, Briget Palmer,
Justine Poole, Christine Sheppard, Angela Tregonning

Published by Murdoch Books Pty Limited

Designer: Michelle Cutler (internals); Marylouise Brammer (cover)
Photographers: Jared Fowler (chapter openers); Stuart Scott (cover)
Stylists: Cherise Koch; (chapter openers); Louise Bickle (cover)
Editor: Gordana Trifunovic Production: Elizabeth Malcolm

Chief Executive: Juliet Rogers
Publishing Director: Kay Scarlett
Commissioning Editor: Lynn Lewis
Senior Designer: Heather Menzies

National Library of Australia Cataloguing-in-Publication Data
Title: Fast food/editor, Lynn Lewis. ISBN 9781741964165 (pbk.)
Series: New chunky. Includes index. Subjects: Quick and easy cookery. 641.555

Printed by 1010 Printing Co.
PRINTED IN CHINA
First printed 2003. This edition 2009.

For fan-forced ovens, set the oven temperature to 20°C (35°F) lower than indicated in the recipe.
We have used 20 ml tablespoon measures. IMPORTANT: Those who might be at risk from the effects
of salmonella poisoning (the elderly, pregnant women, young children and those suffering from immune
deficiency diseases) should consult their GP with any concerns about eating raw eggs.

Cover credits: Cutlery, White Home. littala black-and-white print plates, Design Mode International.
Marimekko Nuppa fabric in colour 101, Chee Soon & Fitzgerald. Hopsack woven fabric and
Peony Garden crewel embroidered fabric, No Chintz. French wine glasses, Ici et la.
Floral print fabric, Spotlight. Front flap: Florence Broadhurst floral print fabric, No Chintz.

A catalogue record for this book is available from the British Library.

Published by:
AUSTRALIA
Murdoch Books Pty Ltd
Pier 8/9, 23 Hickson Road,
Millers Point NSW 2000
Phone: + 61 (0) 2 8220 2000
Fax: + 61 (0) 2 8220 2558
www.murdochbooks.com.au

UK
Murdoch Books UK Ltd
Erico House, 6th Floor North,
93-99 Upper Richmond Rd,
Putney, London SW15 2TG
Phone: + 44 (0) 20 8785 5995
Fax: + 44 (0) 20 8785 5985
www.murdochbooks.co.uk